The Natural Remedy Lab

Indian home remedies and the science behind them

TANIKA DAHAD

Roseworks Publishing

Published by Roseworks Publishing

First paperback edition, 2021

Book design by Hyphen Design

ISBN: 978-1-3999-0427-8

www.naturalremedylab.co.uk

To my Dadiji (grandmother),
who always has a remedy for everything

CONTENTS

PAGE

Introduction 01

How to use this book 03

01 Ear & Eye Remedies 04

Earache 06
Earwax Buildup or Blocked Ears 07
Dry, Sore or Irritated Eyes 08
Styes & Chalazia 11

02 Cardiovascular & Respiratory Remedies 12

Angina 14
Asthma 19
Cough or Sore Throat 21
Congestion 26
Hiccups 29
High Blood Pressure 31

03 Hair & Scalp Remedies 34

Dandruff 36
Dry, Frizzy or Damaged Hair 40
Hair Loss & Thinning 42
Head Lice 44

04 Dental Remedies 46

Bad Breath 48
Gum Infection 51
Toothache 53
Ulcers (Canker Sores) 57

05 Skin Remedies 62

Acne & Breakouts 64
Burns 74
Corns & Calluses 79
Cuts & Bruises 81
Chapped or Dry Lips 85
Dark Circles & Puffy Eyes 90
Dry Skin 93
Enlarged Pores 97
Redness & Inflammation 100
Scars & Hyperpigmentation 105

06 Musculoskeletal Remedies 110

Joint Pain & Arthritis 112
Muscle Soreness & Cramps 124

07 Metabolic & Endocrine Remedies 130

Overweight 132
Underweight 136
High Blood Sugar 140
High Cholesterol 143
Thyroid Disease 146

08 **Immune System Remedies** **148**

Weak Immune System 150
Hay Fever 158

09 **Digestive & Urinary Remedies** **162**

Constipation 164
Diarrhoea 168
Gassiness & Bloating 174
Heartburn 178
Stomach Ache or Pain 185
Urinary Tract Infections (UTIs) 189
Urinary Incontinence 191
Vomiting & Nausea 194

10 **Miscellaneous Remedies** **200**

Fatigue 202
Headaches & Migraines 206
Insect Bites 208
Insomnia 211
Loss of Appetite 217
Menstrual Cramps (Dysmenorrhoea) 220

Bibliography 224

Index 225

About the author 232

Introduction

I never planned to write a book, least of all on this topic. My intention was simply to spend some quality time with my dadi (grandma), hear her stories and capture them for future generations. Now, with university finally over and all the extra free time arising from the pandemic, this was my chance.

During my childhood, I had heard many anecdotes from my dadi of various folk knowledge and remedies, but there was no real coherence or structure to them in my head, except that most of them involved turmeric (or "haldi" as we call it in Hindi) – the yellow-orange spice used as a remedy for everything (except of course for whitening your teeth).

I also have to admit that I didn't pay much attention at the time, as I was a healthy child who didn't really have a use for any of this information. However, having dealt with unpleasant side effects from prescribed medication since being diagnosed with Crohn's disease in 2016, I began to appreciate the benefit of managing my health more holistically.

In the summer of 2020, my horizons began to expand beyond turmeric. My dadi was drawing on her vast knowledge base acquired from being brought up by her nani (maternal grandmother) in rural India in the 1940s, who, despite not being able to read or write, used to provide herbal medicine to people in her village for free. I was in awe of the fact that here was information being passed down to me from four generations ago – from my great-great-grandmother – and who knows how much further back some of these remedies might have originated. My dadi also continued in her nani's footsteps since moving to England in 1968, helping friends and family with these remedies, some of which she added to or adapted based on what was available here.

However, was there any basis or evidence for any of these remedies actually working? At the time of writing, my dadi remains remarkably healthy for an octogenarian. She has had no need for any prescribed medication for as long as I can remember and has just walked a hundred kilometres in one month to raise money for a local charity for kidney patients. Her good health may serve as testimony to the remedies she has used for years, or it may be sufficient that she believes they work.

I nevertheless began my research while donning my sceptic's hat, as Dadi's case – whilst impressive – is only anecdotal. There was sufficient doubt in my mind to explore the rationale for some of her remedies and to try to find any scientific evidence for each one of them. The initial motivation was to develop an understanding of these remedies before subjecting my body to any of them, to understand what effect (if any) they would have on me if I were to use them.

This book is the end result of abstracting my notes into something that I can easily reference. I hope you can also derive some benefit from my research. Perhaps you have been using some of the remedies in this book already, in which case you can draw some comfort in the fact that there may be some science behind them. In general, I have included only those remedies for which I was able to find published research pointing to their potential benefits, which remarkably, was most of them.

How to use this book

This book can be read cover to cover or used as a reference book for specific ailments, either by using the main contents page or using the index to search by ailment or ingredient.

These natural home remedies have a long history of use in India, and there's a reason they have persisted for so long – this is where the science comes in. For each remedy, its effectiveness and how it works is explained via the findings of high-quality research from peer-reviewed journals. If you want to dive deeper, the research for each remedy has been referenced at the end of the book, categorised by ailment.

Equipped with the knowledge of how each natural ingredient works for different problems, this book will allow you to take your health into your own hands, maybe even creating your own remedies, mixing and matching ingredients to suit your needs.

The intention of this book is to include remedies with common, easy to find ingredients – whether it be at supermarkets, your local health shop, pharmacy, or online (e.g. Amazon). All ingredients should also be easy to find at an Indian grocery store, though some may not have easy access to one of these.

It's important to note that this book is not an exhaustive guide for every natural Indian remedy, especially as a number of them involve ingredients that are not so accessible in the Western world.

Disclaimer

This book is for informational purposes, and is not a replacement for professional medical advice and treatment. The author of this book is not a herbal expert or medical professional. Information in this book was written with the greatest possible care and accuracy. This however, does not exclude possibility of information becoming outdated due to research developments, nor does it provide any guarantee of effectiveness. The author does not accept responsibility for loss, harm or damage from the use or misuse of this book or failure to seek proper medical advice.

- Any external remedies should be patch tested 12-24 hours before use to check for allergies. You can patch test on the inside of your elbow, behind or just in front of the ear, the underside of the jaw, or another small patch of skin.

- Do not use any remedies on children under the age of 2 years without first consulting a medical professional.

- Consult a medical professional before using any remedies if you are pregnant, nursing, taking medication(s) or undergoing treatment for any pre-existing condition(s).

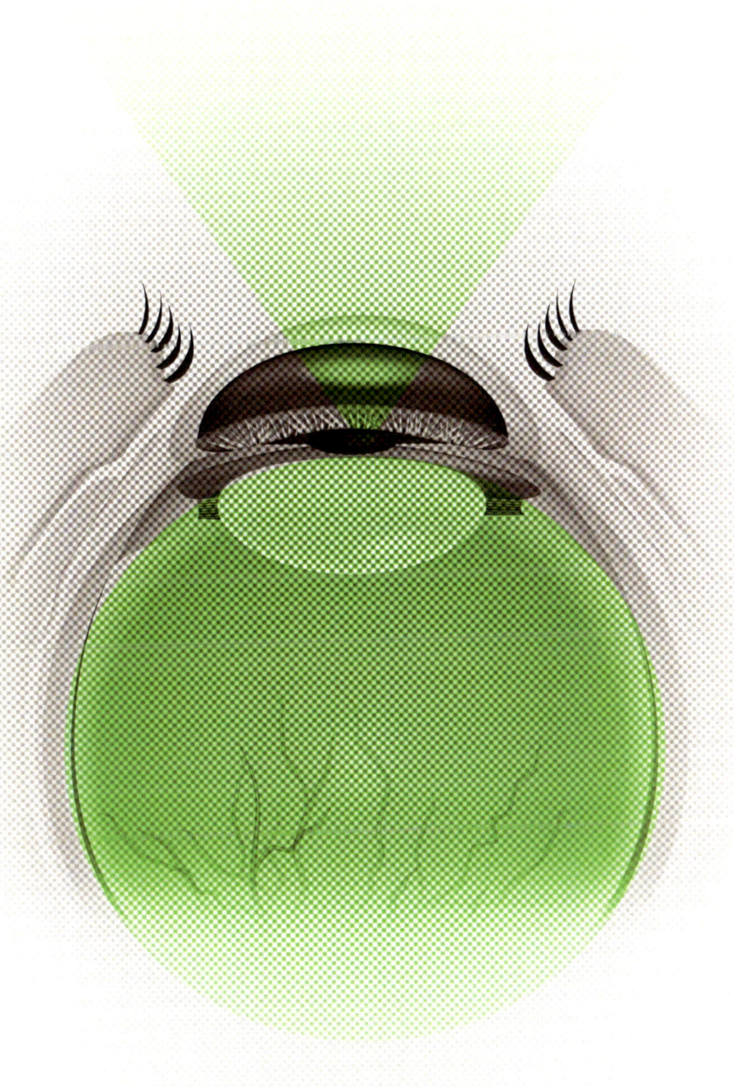

Ear & Eye

Ear & Eye Remedies

PAGE 06 Earache

PAGE 07 Earwax Buildup or Blocked Ears

PAGE 08 Dry, Sore or Irritated Eyes

PAGE 11 Styes & Chalazia

Earache

Garlic Oil Ear Drops

1 clove garlic, chopped
2-4 tbsp olive oil

1. Add the chopped garlic to a pan with the olive oil.
2. Warm the mixture over low heat just until fragrant. Make sure the oil doesn't smoke or bubble.
3. Let the mixture cool and strain out the garlic pieces.
4. Lie on one side with the affected ear facing up. Put 2-3 drops of the warm garlic oil into the ear and stay in position for 10-15 minutes. You can alternatively soak a piece of cotton in the garlic oil and rest it inside the ear so the oil seeps into the ear canal.

NOTE

Store the remaining oil in a glass jar or dropper bottle in the fridge for up to 3 days. To reheat or warm the mixture, put the bottle of garlic oil in a bowl of hot water for 1-2 minutes. Test on your hand before using to make sure it's not too hot.

CAUTION

Do not use this if you have a perforated eardrum

FREQUENCY

No more than 2-3 times a day

Studies have found garlic to be effective at treating earache or ear pain. Garlic has antiviral, antibacterial, antifungal, anti-inflammatory and pain-relieving properties, due to components like allicin and quercetin. These properties can help fight ear infections (a common cause of earache) and ease the pain.

Earwax Buildup or Blocked Ears

½ tsp baking soda/bicarbonate of soda
50 ml lukewarm water

1. Add the baking soda to the lukewarm water and mix well.
2. Lie on one side, and add 5-10 drops of the mixture in the problem ear.
3. Leave to settle for a few minutes, then shake out.

CAUTION

Do not use this if you have a perforated eardrum

FREQUENCY

Once should be enough, but if the problem persists then use once daily for a few more days

Bicarbonate of soda is alkaline while ear wax is acidic, so the drops will soften and gently dissolve hardened earwax.

Dry, Sore or Irritated Eyes

Ginger & Honey Eye Drops

1 drop root ginger juice
3 drops honey
15 drops or 0.75 ml sterilised water
(to sterilise water, boil for 20 minutes)

1. Mix the root ginger juice with the honey.
2. Add the sterilised water to mixture and leave the mixture to cool completely.
3. Apply 1 drop in each eye using an eye drop bottle, clean fingers or a pipette.
4. Close your eyes for a few seconds, then blink and let your eyes water.

NOTE

Stinging is to be expected on application, but this will not last for long. If the discomfort continues or gets worse after 10-15 minutes then wash your eyes with cold water. If this still doesn't help then contact your doctor.

CAUTION

Wait at least 30 minutes after application before inserting contact lenses

FREQUENCY

No more than once a day

Root ginger juice contains anti-inflammatory and analgesic agents which can soothe pain and reduce corneal inflammation.

Honey has anti-inflammatory and antimicrobial properties which have been shown to be effective in treating corneal dryness and inflammation, corneal ulcers, conjunctivitis and various bacterial eye infections.

Rose Water Compress

This is especially helpful if the irritation is due to heat or too much screen time.

Rose water
2 cotton pads

1. Soak the cotton pads in rose water.
   For added relief, leave the rosewater-soaked cotton pads in the refrigerator for 10 minutes before use.
2. Leave on eyes for at least 10 minutes.

FREQUENCY

As often as needed

Rose water has anti-inflammatory and antihistaminic properties which help to soothe sore eyes and reduce irritation. It also has anti-infective properties, which can help with problems like dacryocystitis (infection of the tear sacs).

Rose Water Drops

For eye dryness, redness or inflammation, this may be more helpful than a compress.

1. Add 1-2 drops of rose water to the affected eye.

If removing dust or foreign particles:

2. Gently rub your eye for a couple of seconds after applying the drops.
3. Rinse your eye with cold or warm water.

If not removing anything:

2. Sit with your eyes closed for a couple of minutes after applying the drops, then open.

FREQUENCY

Up to 3 times a day for no more than a week

Styes & Chalazia

The remedies on pages 8-10 can also be used for styes and chalazia. They can be accompanied with a warm compress over the affected eye for 5-10 minutes up to 4 times a day to help the stye drain and heal faster.

Turmeric Water

This can also be used for any eye infection.

½ tsp ground turmeric
1 cup water

1. Put the turmeric in a glass of water but don't stir it.
2. Let the turmeric settle at the bottom of the glass (this takes about 20 minutes).
3. Using your finger or a cotton swab, dab some of the turmeric-infused water (but not the turmeric from the bottom of the glass) in the lower waterline of your eyes.

NOTE

If the stye is external, you can also soak a cotton pad or cloth in warm turmeric water and use it as a compress for your eyes.

FREQUENCY

Twice a day – morning and night

> Turmeric can help reduce inflammation in the eyes and has been shown to be effective against infections like conjunctivitis. The curcumin in turmeric also has antibacterial properties which help prevent or remedy any further infection in the eye.

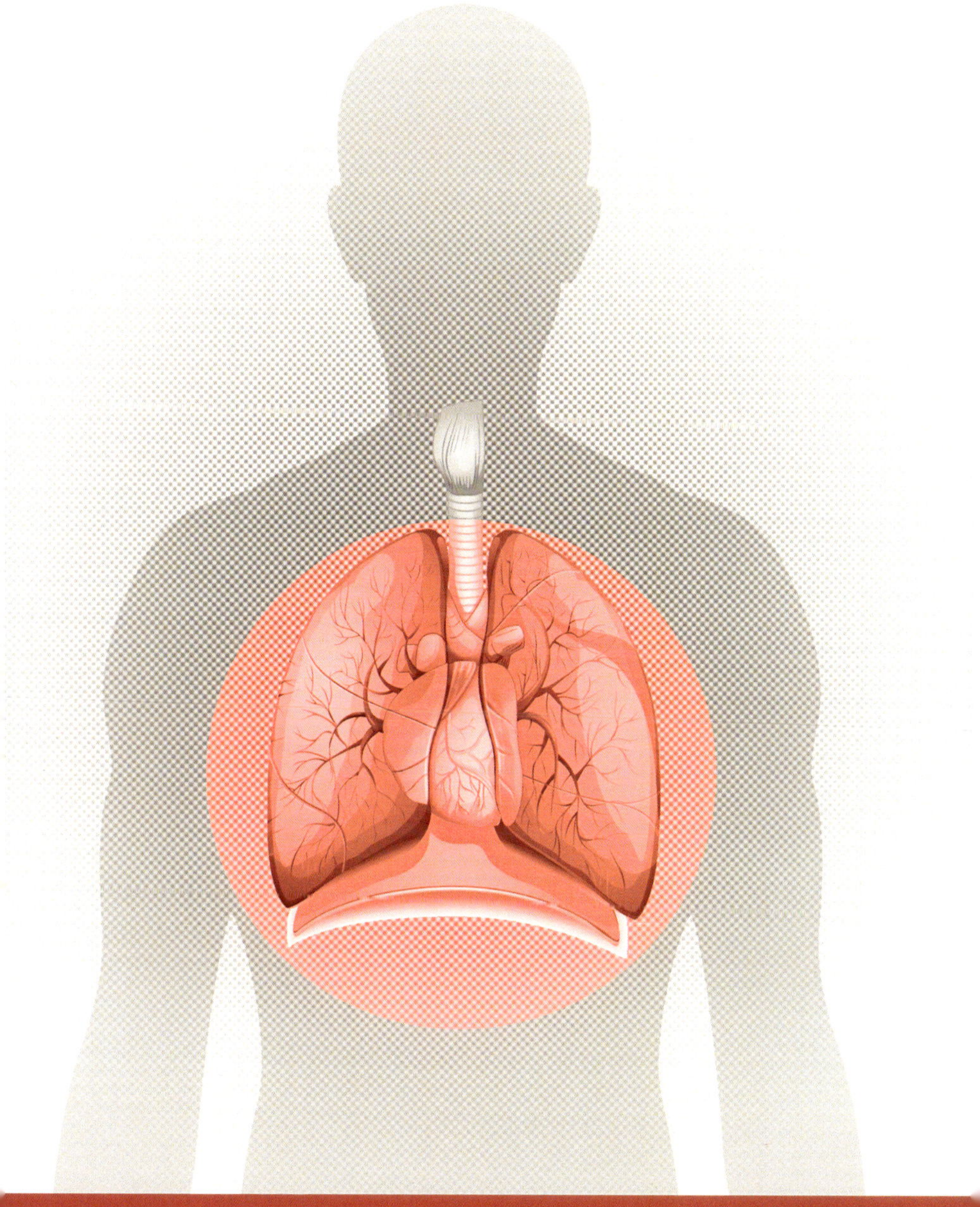

Cardiovascular & Respiratory

Cardiovascular & Respiratory

PAGE 14 Angina

PAGE 19 Asthma

PAGE 21 Cough or Sore Throat

PAGE 26 Congestion

PAGE 29 Hiccups

PAGE 31 High Blood Pressure

Angina

Target Cholesterol

High cholesterol can lead to atherosclerosis – a build-up of fatty deposits (plaques) inside the arteries – which can slow down blood flow, causing angina and other symptoms of coronary artery disease.

See pages 143-145 for remedies that target high cholesterol.

Target Blood Pressure

High blood pressure can damage artery walls due to the increased force of blood through the arteries, leading to a decrease in blood and oxygen flow to the heart, resulting in heart disease or symptoms such as angina.

See pages 31-33 for remedies that target high blood pressure.

Target Blood Sugar

Long-term high blood sugar can damage the lining of arterial walls and lead to the development of atherosclerosis as the body can't utilise all the sugar. High blood sugar levels have also been found to lead to blood vessel contraction, which can result in higher blood pressure and a reduced blood and oxygen supply to the heart.

See pages 140-142 for remedies that target high blood sugar.

Garlic Drink

1-2 garlic cloves, chopped
1 cup low-fat milk OR water
1 tbsp honey (optional)

1 Bring the milk or water to a simmer in a pan.

2 Add the garlic and honey and mix well.

3 Remove from heat and leave for 10 minutes.

4 Strain the milk and drink warm.

FREQUENCY

Once daily

SHORTCUT

You can also swallow 1-2 whole garlic cloves with some water.

Garlic has been shown to reduce cholesterol and the progression of atherosclerosis (a build-up of fatty deposits inside the arteries), therefore helping to prevent the slowing or blockage of blood flow that can cause angina. Garlic has also been found to reduce high blood pressure, as it's sulphur-containing components help to relax blood vessels.

Golden Milk

Quantities below are for 2 servings.

1-2 tsp ground turmeric
¼ tsp ground black pepper
½ inch fresh ginger, grated
½ tsp ground cinnamon (optional)
2 cups low-fat milk (for dairy-free, use coconut, almond or soy milk)

1. Add the milk to a pan over medium heat.
2. When the milk is warm, add the turmeric, ground black pepper, ginger and cardamom.
3. Simmer on low heat for 5 minutes.
4. Strain into a mug and drink.

FREQUENCY

Once daily

NOTE

You may get a film or 'skin' on top of the milk as it cools in the mug, but you can just remove this with a spoon or push it to the side.

You can even use water instead of milk (though it won't be as tasty).

SHORTCUT

You can add the turmeric, black pepper, honey and cinnamon (if using) to the milk and heat it all up in the microwave, though you'll miss out on the benefits of the ginger.

Turmeric contains curcumin, which has been found to reduce inflammation and improve endothelial (blood vessel lining) dysfunction – this is important as inflammation and endothelial dysfunction are major drivers of heart disease and chest pain. Curcumin has also been shown to reduce 'bad' LDL cholesterol whilst increasing 'good' HDL cholesterol, which can help to prevent atherosclerosis.

Black pepper increases the bioavailability of curcumin in turmeric by up to 2000% i.e. improves the absorption of curcumin, as curcumin is otherwise poorly absorbed by the body.

Ginger has been shown to reduce blood pressure by acting as a natural calcium channel blocker and ACE inhibitor, which are the same mechanisms as various blood pressure medications.

Cinnamon helps to relax and dilate blood vessels, and whilst the exact mechanism is unknown, it has been shown to effectively reduce high blood pressure.

Honey Water

1-2 tsp honey
1 cup water

1. Warm the cup of water in a microwave or kettle.
2. Stir in the honey until dissolved.
3. Drink on an empty stomach in the morning.

FREQUENCY

Once daily

Where possible, try to replace sugar in your diet with honey.

Honey has been shown to reduce blood pressure and the risk of heart disease, due to its abundance of antioxidant compounds. It has also been found to reduce blood triglyceride (a type of fat) levels, and reduce 'bad' LDL cholesterol whilst raising 'good' HDL cholesterol. This helps to prevent or slow atherosclerosis, and therefore reduce the risk of angina as blood flow becomes less restricted.

Asthma

Ginger Tea

1 inch fresh ginger, thinly sliced
1-2 cups of water

1. Bring the water to a boil in a saucepan.
2. Add the sliced ginger to the saucepan.
3. Simmer for 5 minutes on low heat. You can leave it for longer for stronger tea.
4. Pour the tea through a sieve to strain out the ginger.
5. Drink the tea.

FREQUENCY

Up to 3 times daily

You can add some honey after straining out the ginger to sweeten the taste.

Research suggests ginger can help reduce the airway inflammation associated with asthma and inhibit airway contraction. Ginger has also been shown to have bronchial relaxation properties.

Turmeric Honey

1-2 tsp ground turmeric
¼ tsp black pepper
3 tbsp honey

1. Mix the turmeric and honey to make a paste.
2. Take 1-2 tsp of this paste daily. You can take it by itself, add it to hot water, or even spread it on toast.

FREQUENCY
Daily

NOTE
Store in an airtight container in the fridge for up to 3 weeks.

Turmeric has been found to help reduce airway obstruction and inflammation, due to the anti-inflammatory, immunomodulatory component in turmeric called curcumin.

Black pepper increases the bioavailability of curcumin in turmeric by up to 2000% i.e. improves the absorption of curcumin.

Honey also has anti-inflammatory properties, which can help reduce airway inflammation. It has also been found more effective than over-the-counter medications for easing coughing – a common symptom of asthma.

Cough Or Sore Throat

Golden Milk

1-2 tsp ground turmeric
¼ tsp ground black pepper
½ inch fresh ginger, grated
½-1 tsp honey (adjust to taste)
2-4 cardamom pods, crushed OR
½ tsp ground cardamom (optional)
2 cups milk (for dairy-free, use coconut, almond or soy milk)

1. Add the milk to a pan over medium heat.
2. When the milk is warm, add the turmeric, ground black pepper, ginger and cardamom.
3. Simmer on low heat for 5 minutes.
4. Strain into a mug and drink.

FREQUENCY

Drink daily - morning & night

SHORTCUT

You can add the turmeric, black pepper and honey to the milk and heat it all up in the microwave, though you'll miss out on the benefits of the ginger.

NOTE

You may get a film or 'skin' over the top as it cools in the mug, but you can just remove this with a spoon or push it to the side.

You can even use water instead of milk (though it won't be as tasty).

Turmeric contains curcumin, which studies suggest have anti-inflammatory effects comparable to pharmaceutical drugs without the side effects. This can therefore help with irritation or inflammation of the airways. It also has antibacterial, antiviral and antioxidant properties, which can help fight infections that might be causing the cough or sore throat.

Black pepper improves the absorption of the curcumin in turmeric by up to 2000%, is anti-inflammatory, and is also rich in an antioxidant called piperine.

Ginger also has anti-inflammatory, antioxidant, and antimicrobial properties and has been shown to boost the immune system. Compounds in fresh ginger have also been found to fight respiratory syncytial virus (RSV) – a common cause of respiratory infections.

Honey is anti-inflammatory, an expectorant (clears mucus), antibiotic and notably, has been found to be more effective at treating coughs and sore throats than over-the-counter medicines and antibiotics.

Spoonful of Sugar

Take a pinch of sugar in your mouth, let it dissolve for a few seconds, then swallow.

Research has shown that crystalline sugar placed on the tongue and then swallowed can suppress coughing by inhibiting the respiratory reflex related to coughing. The sweet taste can also induce analgesia i.e. relieves pain.

Garlic Rub

This is especially helpful for relieving coughing and congestion when trying to sleep.

6 garlic cloves, chopped
3 tbsp olive oil OR coconut oil
5-10 drops lavender oil (optional but helps with the smell as well as your sleep)

For sensitive or baby's skin:

1. Put the garlic and oil into a small jar.
2. Let it infuse for 8-12 hours.
3. Strain well so you are left with the oil.
4. Rub the infused oil onto the chest, back and optionally – the soles of your feet.

For normal skin:

1. Blend the garlic and oil together in a food processor or blender until it is completely smooth – like a butter.
2. Store in a glass jar.
3. Rub onto the chest, back and optionally – the soles of your feet.

FREQUENCY

Every 2-3 hours or as needed

Wear an old t-shirt and socks to protect your bed or furniture smelling like garlic.

Garlic, when freshly crushed or chopped, contains an antimicrobial compound called allicin, which can help fight infections that may be causing the cough. Garlic also acts as an expectorant, helping to thin the mucus that might be causing congestion and productive coughs.

Minty Lemongrass & Ginger Drink

6 mint leaves
1-2 lemongrass stalks, quartered
1 tsp grated ginger
2 cups water OR milk
1 tsp sugar OR honey (optional)

1. Bring the water or milk to a boil in a saucepan.
2. Add all the remaining ingredients and simmer for 5-7 minutes.
3. Strain into a cup and drink.

CAUTION

Do not drink if you suffer from low blood pressure

FREQUENCY

Up to 3 times a day

You can add a few pinches of ground turmeric for added benefits.

Mint leaves contain menthol, which helps to numb nerve endings in the throat that become irritated from coughing, and can therefore provide pain relief and reduce the urge to cough. Mint has also been found to reduce congestion by breaking down mucus, and has antibacterial and antiviral properties which can help fight infections that might be causing the cough or congestion.

Lemongrass has anti-inflammatory properties, which can help to reduce irritation or inflammation of the airways. Lemongrass also contains several flavonoids which act as antioxidants, and can therefore protect against damage to immune cells, helping the body fight infections and easing cough and cold symptoms.

Ginger has anti-inflammatory, antioxidant, and antimicrobial properties and has been shown to boost the immune system. Compounds in fresh ginger have also been found to fight respiratory syncytial virus (RSV) – a common cause of respiratory infections.

Congestion

Garlic Nasal Drops

1 garlic clove, chopped
½ cup water
¼ tsp salt (to avoid burning sensation)
1 dropper bottle OR pipette

1. Add the salt to the water and boil in a pan for 15 minutes.
2. Switch off the heat and when the water stops bubbling, add the garlic to the pan.
3. Stir the mixture until fragrant.
4. Allow the mixture to cool to room temperature, then strain out the garlic pieces so you're left with the liquid.
5. Lie on a bed or sofa and hang your head back over the edge. Put 1-2 drops of the liquid in each nostril using a dropper bottle or pipette.
6. Stay in this position for two minutes so the liquid doesn't run out of the nose or down the back of the throat. You may get a garlicky taste in your mouth after using the drops but that's normal.

FREQUENCY

Up to twice a day for no more than 3 days

NOTE

This can be stored in an airtight container in the fridge for up to 24 hours.

Garlic is naturally antimicrobial, due to its bioactive compounds like allicin, and can therefore help to fight infections that might be causing colds and congestion. It also acts as an expectorant, helping to thin the mucus blocking nasal passages.

Golden Milk

See pages 21-22 for recipe and explanation.

Garlic Rub

See pages 23-24 for recipe and explanation.

Minty Lemongrass & Ginger Drink

See pages 24-25 for recipe and explanation.

Steam Inhalation

1 large bowl
Water
1 tbsp mint leaves, roughly chopped OR
½ tsp Vicks Vaporub

1. Boil the water.
2. Pour the hot water into the bowl until about half full
3. Stir in the mint leaves or Vicks.
4. Place your face over the bowl with a towel over your head to trap the steam. Be careful not to put your face too close to the steam.
5. Close your eyes and take deep breaths through your nose for 10-15 minutes.
6. Blow your nose afterwards to get rid of any loosened mucus.

FREQUENCY

You can do this 2-3 times daily

You can add more mint leaves if the scent isn't strong enough.

Inhaling hot steam has been shown to help treat congestion by opening the airways and dislodging mucus.

Mint contains menthol, a compound found to stimulate cold receptors in the nose and throat, which cools and soothes the airway passages, giving the feeling of a clear, open nose. Mint also has antibacterial properties which have been shown to fight respiratory tract pathogens.

Hiccups

Ginger

½ inch of ginger, thinly sliced
1 cup water

OR

1 small piece of ginger

1. Bring the water to a boil in a saucepan.
2. Add the sliced ginger to the pan.
3. Simmer for 5 minutes on low heat.
4. Pour the tea through a sieve to strain out the ginger.
5. Take small sips until you finish the drink.

OR

1. Put the ginger in your mouth.
2. Suck on it for 5 minutes, then swallow or discard.

Ginger has anti-inflammatory properties which can relax the diaphragm muscle or help with hiccups caused by indigestion. The strong taste of ginger could also stimulate the vagus nerve, thus helping the diaphragm to relax.

Holding Water

1 cup water

1 Take a sip of cold water but don't swallow it – try to hold it at the back of your throat, almost so it's blocking the opening.

2 Hold it there as long as you can then gently swallow the water (don't gulp).

3 Repeat until the hiccups have gone.

This remedy forces you to hold your breath, as this can stop the involuntary contractions of the diaphragm by mildly raising the body's CO_2 levels. Researchers are unsure why this works – some suggest it distracts the body to deal with the build-up of CO_2, or that hiccups are caused by low CO_2 in the first place.

High Blood Pressure

If your high blood pressure is due to obesity or overweight, then see pages 132-135. The remedies on pages 14-18 may also be helpful.

Pranayama (Savasana)

1. Lie on your back with arms and legs stretched out
2. Take a deep breath in and hold for 10-15 seconds, then exhale slowly. Repeat for 5 minutes.
3. Then turn on your left hand side for one minute before getting up.

FREQUENCY

Twice daily – morning and evening

NOTE

This should not be done immediately after eating.

> Research has shown pranayama to be effective in reducing blood pressure, with one study finding it as effective as medical therapy. This could be due to the breath exercises promoting relaxation, which reduces the body's stress response and therefore the risk of hypertension. The slow and deep breathing also leads to vasodilation and therefore a drop in blood pressure.

Pranayama (Anulom Vilom)

1 Take a deep breath in through your left nostril whilst closing your right nostril with your thumb.

2 Hold for a few seconds, then breathe out through your right nostril whilst closing your left nostril with two fingers.

3 Then, breathe in through your right nostril, hold, and exhale through your left nostril.

FREQUENCY

Repeat this process for 10 minutes every day

Watermelon & Basil Drink

½ watermelon
4 basil leaves
1 pinch black pepper
1 tbsp fresh lime juice (adjust to taste)
2 mint leaves (optional – adjust to taste)

1 Chop the watermelon and remove any seeds.

2 Place all the ingredients into a blender and blend until smooth. Add a little water if needed.

3 Pour into a glass and drink.

FREQUENCY

Once daily

NOTE

This can be stored in the fridge for 1-2 days.

You can substitute watermelon for unsweetened pomegranate or carrot juice.

Watermelon contains lycopene, a potent antioxidant which has been found to lower blood pressure by reducing the stiffness and thickness of artery walls. Watermelon also contains citrulline, which increases nitric oxide levels, which helps to expand blood vessels, and therefore lower blood pressure.

Basil is rich in antioxidants including eugenol, which helps to reduce blood pressure by acting as a natural calcium channel blocker i.e. it prevents the movement of calcium into the heart and arterial cells, which allows the blood vessels to relax.

Black pepper contains piperine, a bioactive compound that has been found to lower blood pressure and help with vasomodulation (regulating blood flow), though the underlying mechanism for this is unclear.

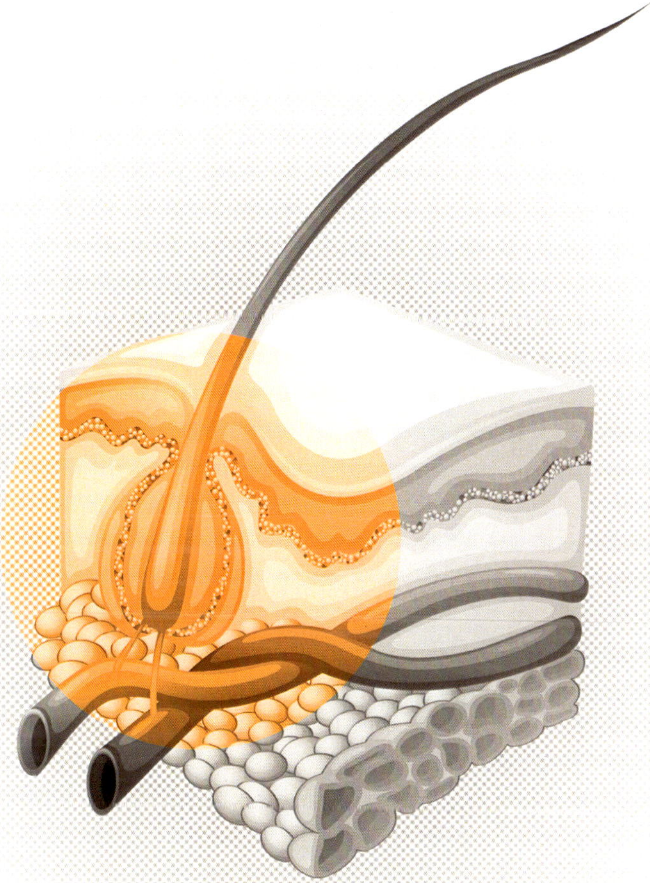

Hair & Scalp

Hair & Scalp Remedies

PAGE 36 Dandruff

PAGE 40 Dry, Frizzy or Damaged Hair

PAGE 42 Hair Loss & Thinning

PAGE 44 Head Lice

Dandruff

Sour Yoghurt & Lemon Hair Mask

4-5 tbsp yoghurt OR buttermilk
1-2 tbsp lemon juice

1. To make the sour yoghurt, leave the yoghurt out in a warm place for a couple of days until it tastes sour (but stir it each day to make sure mould doesn't form on the surface).

   NOTE

   If using buttermilk, you don't need to leave it out as it already has a higher lactic acid content than yoghurt. Simply mix it with the lemon juice and go to step 3.

2. Mix together the sour yoghurt and lemon juice.
3. Before you shower, massage the mixture into your scalp and hair for a couple of minutes then wash your hair as normal.

CAUTION

If you have eczema or psoriasis, you may want to reduce or remove the lemon juice as the citric acid can potentially cause irritation

FREQUENCY

2-3 times a week until the dandruff has gone

The lactic acid in the yoghurt or buttermilk can help to gently exfoliate the scalp and clear away the dead skin cells, dandruff flakes and excess sebum, whilst the protein and fat in the yoghurt help to strengthen hair follicles and moisturise the scalp and hair. Leaving the yoghurt out allows further fermentation, therefore increasing the lactic acid content (hence why it goes sour).

The citric acid in lemon juice acts as a natural pH adjuster for the scalp by absorbing excess oil and sebum (a common cause of dandruff), which is why shampoos often include citric fruits. Lemon is also rich in vitamin B, which has been found to improve skin conditions like seborrheic dermatitis – a trigger for dandruff.

Neem Water Rinse

10-20 neem leaves OR 1 tbsp neem leaf powder
2 litres water

1. Boil the neem leaves in the water until the water becomes greenish, then allow to cool. If using powder, boil the water, remove from heat, then stir in the powder until dissolved.
2. Strain the water into a container or dispenser you can use in the bath or shower.
3. After shampooing your hair, rinse your scalp and hair with this neem water.

FREQUENCY

2-3 times a week until the dandruff has gone

Neem leaves have anti-bacterial, anti-fungal and anti-inflammatory (due to nimbidin) properties which therefore help to address a number of the root causes of dandruff, such as irritated skin on the scalp due to dermatitis or psoriasis, and Malassezia (fungus).

Homemade Neem Oil Massage

2 tbsp neem leaf powder
1 cup coconut oil
2 tsp lemon juice

1. Mix the neem leaf powder with melted coconut oil.
2. Leave this mixture for 2-4 hours or put the mixture in a glass container and place in a pan of boiling water for 15 mins.
3. Leave to cool then strain so you're left with the oil, then add the lemon juice to the oil.
4. Massage the oil into your scalp.
5. Leave in for at least 2 hours but ideally overnight.
6. Wash your hair as usual (you may need to repeat the shampoo step to get all the oil out).

CAUTION

If you have eczema or psoriasis, you may want to reduce or remove the lemon juice as the citric acid can potentially cause irritation

FREQUENCY

No more than once a week as you don't want to risk making your scalp oilier, especially if you have seborrheic dermatitis

SHORTCUT

Buy neem oil and mix with lemon juice (and coconut oil if desired), then follow steps 4 to 6.

Put a dry towel over your pillow if leaving the oil on overnight so that it doesn't stain your pillowcase.

Neem leaves have anti-bacterial, anti-fungal and anti-inflammatory (due to nimbidin) properties which therefore help to address a number of the root causes of dandruff, such as irritated skin on the scalp due to dermatitis or psoriasis, and Malassezia (fungus).

Coconut oil has anti-fungal, antimicrobial, anti-inflammatory and moisturising properties due to the presence of medium-chain fatty acids like lauric acid. Clinical studies support its efficacy in treating dermatitis and fungus (some of the causes of dandruff) and its properties may help to combat other dandruff-causing skin conditions like psoriasis.

The citric acid in lemon juice acts as a natural pH adjuster for the scalp by absorbing excess oil and sebum (a common cause of dandruff), which is why shampoos often include citric fruits. Lemon is also rich in vitamin B, which has been found to improve skin conditions like seborrheic dermatitis – a trigger for dandruff.

Dry, Frizzy or Damaged Hair

Oil Massage

2-4 tbsp coconut oil
(quantity depends on your hair length)
Note: jojoba or olive oil will also work well
1 towel or shower cap

1. Warm the coconut oil in your hands and massage it into your scalp and hair.
2. Wrap your hair in a shower cap or damp towel for at least 30-45 minutes, or leave oil overnight for a deeper conditioning.
3. Wash off with shampoo (you may need to shampoo twice to get all the oil out).

FREQUENCY

1-2 times a week

Put a dry towel over your pillow if leaving the oil on overnight so that it doesn't stain your pillowcase.

> Coconut oil can repair dry or damaged hair by penetrating the hair shaft (more deeply than most oils) and restoring moisture. It can also add shine due to the oil smoothing and sealing the outer cuticle of the hair – this is the layer that locks in moisture. Hair frizzes when water gets into the hair shaft, causing it to swell and become uneven. As oil can penetrate the hair shaft and is hydrophobic (repels water), it helps prevent frizz.

Banana Hair Mask

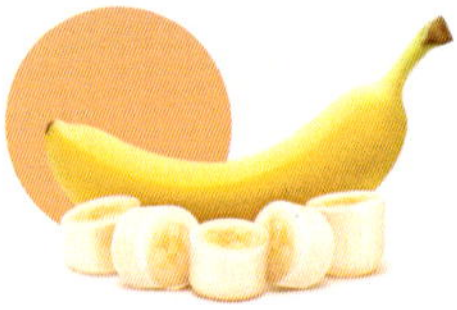

1-2 ripe bananas

1 Mash the bananas and spread it on the hair from roots to ends as a hair mask.

2 Leave it on for one hour and then wash out thoroughly.

NOTE
Ensure the banana is washed out completely as debris left on scalp can cause irritation.

CAUTION

Do not use if you have a latex-fruit allergy

FREQUENCY

1-3 times a week

For a supercharged hair mask you can also add 1 avocado, 1 tbsp honey and 1 tbsp coconut oil to provide further moisture and hydration.

Bananas are rich in vitamin E, natural oils, and potassium, which help to condition dry hair and improve elasticity, therefore making the hair less prone to breakage and split ends. Bananas also contain several antioxidants, which can help fight against free radical damage to the hair resulting from factors like pollution, sunlight, and even stress.

Hair Loss & Thinning

Egg & Coconut Oil Hair Mask

1 egg
1 tbsp coconut oil, melted
1 banana (optional – can help to smooth and moisturise hair)

1. Mix the egg with the coconut oil and stir until you get a smooth mixture.
2. Apply the mixture to hair and scalp, working it in from the roots to the tips with your fingers.
3. Leave on for 20 minutes and wash out thoroughly using shampoo and lukewarm water so that the egg does not solidify.

FREQUENCY

Once a week

Eggs are densely packed with vitamins A and D, biotin, folate and protein. Applying egg to the scalp infuses the hair root with these nutrients, so the new hair will grow out stronger and be less prone to breakage and shredding.

The lauric acid in coconut oil helps bind protein in hair, protecting it from breakage at the root and strand. When the amount of hair falling out is reduced, the body of hair becomes thicker and fuller. Lauric acid has also been shown to block DHT – a hormone linked to hair loss and pattern baldness – in preclinical studies.

Amla Oil Massage

2-4 tbsp amla (Indian gooseberry) oil
(quantity depends on your hair length)

1. Massage the amla oil into the scalp and hair.
2. Leave in for at least an hour, but ideally overnight.
3. Wash off thoroughly with shampoo. You may need to shampoo twice.

FREQUENCY

1-2 times a week

NOTE

This may darken your hair if you have light or blonde hair so patch test first or use another hair oil like argan oil, and mix it with some camphor oil.

Put a dry towel over your pillow if leaving the oil on overnight so that it doesn't stain your pillowcase.

Amla oil has been found to be a powerful inhibitor of 5-alpha reductase, which is how finasteride – medication used to treat male baldness – also works. Amla oil is also rich in vitamin C, which can promote the production of collagen, helping to fight hair follicle damage, build hair proteins & strengthen the skin containing hair roots. The vitamin C can also help the absorption of iron – a mineral necessary for hair growth.

Scalp massage can stimulate hair growth by dilating blood vessels beneath the skin, bringing oxygen and nutrients to the hair follicles, and also increase hair thickness by stretching the cells of hair follicles.

Head Lice

Oil Massage

3 tbsp coconut oil, melted
1 tsp tea tree oil
1 plastic shower cap
1 fine-tooth lice comb
5 drops neem oil OR a neem-based shampoo

1. Mix together the coconut and tea tree oil. You can make more of this mixture in the same ratio if needed.
2. Massage the mixture generously into your scalp and hair.
3. Apply a plastic shower cap and leave this on overnight (for at least 8 hours).
4. Remove the shower cap and comb out the lice and eggs with the lice comb.
5. Wash your hair with a neem-based shampoo (or add 5 drops of neem oil per tbsp of regular shampoo).

FREQUENCY

Repeat every 2-3 days until the lice have gone

NOTE

Before using tea tree oil, put a small drop of the coconut-tea tree oil mixture on the back of your hand and if you have no reaction, you can safely use it. If you do have a reaction then lavender or aniseed oil can be used instead.

Coconut oil suffocates the lice, and contains fatty acids like lauric acid, which make it challenging for lice to grip to hair strands and therefore easier to comb them out.

Tea tree oil has been shown to kill both lice and nits as it contains two major constituents with insecticidal activity: 1,8-cineole and terpinen-4-ol.

Neem has compounds such as azadirachtin which has been found to disrupt the life cycle of the louse, making it a natural insect repellent.

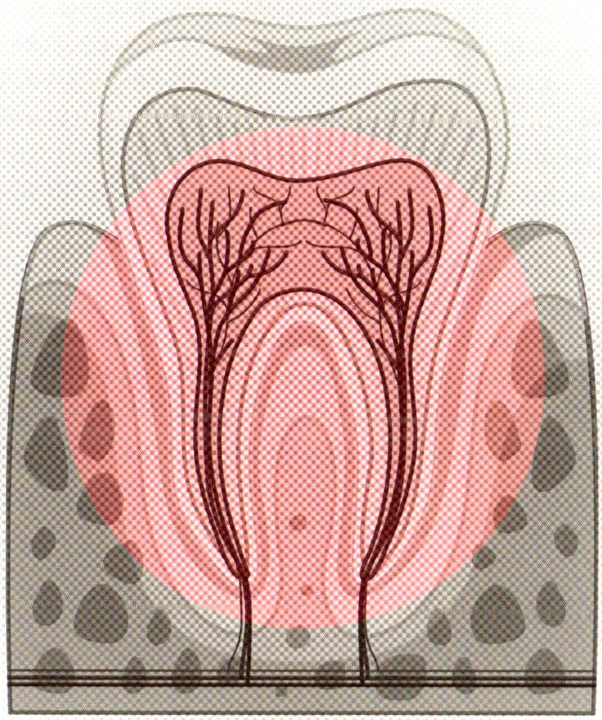

Dental

Dental Remedies

PAGE 48 Bad Breath (Halitosis)

PAGE 51 Gum Infection

PAGE 53 Toothache

PAGE 57 Ulcers (Canker Sores)

Bad Breath (Halitosis)

The most common cause of bad breath is bacteria that grows on bits of food left in your mouth or caught in your teeth. Therefore the main solution is just good dental hygiene i.e. brush and floss twice a day. However, if bad breath is still an issue, then there are some remedies to help with the smell.

Fennel Seed Freshener

1 cup fennel seeds

1. Lightly roast the fennel seeds in a dry pan for 1-2 minutes until golden brown and aromatic.
2. Fill a small container with the roasted seeds to carry with you. Keep any remaining seeds in a jar or container in a cupboard.
3. After you finish eating, chew and swallow a few pinches of the seeds and then drink some water.

FREQUENCY

After meals or as often as needed

NOTE

Any extra seeds that don't fit in the small container can be stored in a jar or container in a cupboard. They can last for around 2 years.

In Indian culture, this is a common mouth freshener to cleanse after-dinner breath. It tastes slightly sweet and contains aromatic essential oils that give the breath a fresh scent. It also has antibacterial properties, which can help cleanse pathogens causing bad breath, and chewing the seeds increases saliva to wash away bacteria in your mouth.

Cinnamon Mouth Rinse

2 tsp ground cinnamon
1 cup water

1. Boil the water in a kettle or pan.
2. Mix in the cinnamon and let cool.
3. Transfer to a glass bottle or jar.
4. Use as a mouth wash by swishing some of the solution around your mouth for at least 30 seconds before spitting out.

FREQUENCY

Up to twice a day

NOTE

Store at room temperature for up to a week.

When out and about you can chew a cinnamon stick instead of gum or a mint.

Cinnamon has potent antibacterial properties due to the presence of cinnamaldehyde, and has been shown to reduce the production of volatile sulphur compounds and bacteria that cause bad breath, such as *S. moorei*.

Water

Aim to drink 8 glasses of water per day to ensure your mouth doesn't dry out.

To encourage yourself to drink more, try different things like using a reusable water bottle that isn't effort to drink from (e.g. doesn't require unscrewing a cap), a bottle with time markings, or set reminders on your phone to drink water.

Research shows that mouth dryness often causes bad breath due to a lack of saliva, which plays an important role in keeping your mouth clean and less hospitable to bad bacteria. Saliva also means you're swallowing more often, which washes away the bacteria in your mouth causing bad breath. Drinking water prevents mouth dryness and lack of saliva.

Gum Infection

Turmeric Gum Massage

¼ tsp ground turmeric

1 Massage the turmeric onto your gums for about 5 minutes.
2 Rinse off the residue with warm water.
3 Repeat this every few hours.

FREQUENCY

2-3 times a day until the infection is gone

Turmeric contains curcumin, which has potent anti-inflammatory and antioxidant properties. Turmeric has been shown by extensive research to be effective in treating gingivitis and the associated redness and swelling of gums.

Daily Dose of Turmeric

This remedy is more effective for prevention rather than treatment of gum disease.

¼ tsp ground turmeric
1 pinch black pepper
1 cup water OR milk
(you can also use coconut, almond or soy milk)

1. Warm the water or milk in a pan or the microwave.
2. Add the turmeric to the warm water or milk and stir until the drink becomes golden-yellow.
3. Drink whilst warm.

FREQUENCY

Twice daily – morning and evening

Toothache

Clove Oil

It's important to find out the cause of your toothache because if it's due to reasons such as a rotten tooth, then a dentist's intervention would be required to remove the tooth and home remedies may not be able to help. Assuming it's minor irritation, the following could help.

Clove oil OR 1 whole clove
1 cotton ball

If using whole clove:

1. Place the clove on the affected tooth.
2. Chew it a little bit to release the oil.

If using clove oil:

1. Soak the cotton ball in a few drops of clove oil.
2. Apply directly to the affected area inside your mouth.

FREQUENCY

Up to 3 times a day

Clove oil contains eugenol, which is a natural antiseptic. It is also a mild anaesthetic, and can numb the nerves in the tooth, therefore alleviating the pain.

Garlic Paste

1 garlic clove
1 pinch salt
1 cotton swab (optional)

1 Make a garlic paste by crushing the garlic clove with a pestle and mortar or the back of a spoon, and mix it with a pinch of salt. If the paste is too dry, you can add a tiny bit of water.

2 Apply the paste to the affected tooth using a cotton swab or your fingers. Make sure not to cram the paste into the tooth as this will just cause more irritation.

FREQUENCY

Once daily until the toothache subsides

> Garlic, when freshly cut or crushed, contains allicin which has antibacterial and antimicrobial properties. This can help kill bacteria associated with toothache, therefore reducing the pain.

Salt Water Rinse

1 tsp salt
½ cup warm water

1. Dissolve the salt in the warm water.
2. Swirl the solution in your mouth for 15 to 30 seconds, then spit out.
3. Repeat until you have finished the water.

FREQUENCY

Every few hours
or as needed

Salt water is a natural disinfectant, and it can help loosen trapped food particles and debris that may be stuck in between your teeth causing irritation. It is also antibacterial and can reduce inflammation.

Cold Compress

1 bag of ice OR other frozen item
e.g. bag of peas
1 towel or cloth

1. Wrap the ice or frozen item in the towel or cloth.
2. Apply the cold compress to the affected area (from the outside of your mouth) for 20 minutes at a time.

FREQUENCY

Every few hours
or as needed

> Cold compresses cause the blood vessels in the area to constrict, which makes the pain less severe and can also reduce swelling and inflammation.

Ulcers (Canker Sores)

Banana Pad

1 slice of banana

1. Mash the banana slice to make a paste or use it whole.
2. Apply to the ulcer and leave for 30 minutes.
3. You can then remove it or swallow it.

CAUTION

Do not use if you have a latex-fruit allergy

FREQUENCY

3 to 4 times daily

> Whilst there is currently no conclusive scientific evidence for the effectiveness of this remedy, bananas have been shown to be beneficial for ulcers within the digestive tract, and also have anti-inflammatory properties. Bananas also have antibacterial compounds which inhibit the growth of *H. pylori* – a bacterium that can cause recurrent mouth ulcers.

Chamomile Compress

1 wet chamomile tea bag

1 Apply the tea bag to the ulcer.

2 Leave it on for 5-10 minutes.

FREQUENCY

3 to 4 times daily

> Chamomile contains two compounds with anti-inflammatory and antiseptic abilities: azulene and levomenol, making it an effective treatment for ulcers.

Honey

Unpasteurised honey (less processed so retains more of its healing properties)

Cotton swab (optional)

1 Apply some honey to the ulcer with a clean finger or a cotton swab.

FREQUENCY

At least 4 times daily

Mix in a pinch of turmeric for added antibacterial and anti-inflammatory effects.

Honey is known for its antibacterial and anti-inflammatory properties, and research has found it to be effective in reducing the pain, size and redness of mouth ulcers, as well as helping to prevent a secondary infection.

Salt Water Rinse

1 tsp salt
½ cup warm water

1 Dissolve the salt in the warm water.
2 Swirl the solution in your mouth for 15 to 30 seconds, then spit out.
3 Repeat until you have finished the water.

FREQUENCY

Every few hours or as needed

> Salt water rinses are well-known and even recommended by dentists as an effective remedy for inflammation and mouth sores. It helps to temporarily increase the pH in your mouth, making it difficult for bacteria to survive.

Ghee & Coconut Oil Ointment

Ghee
Coconut oil

1. Mix equal parts ghee and coconut oil – as much as you need to cover the ulcer.
2. Apply this mixture to the sore.

FREQUENCY

Several times a day until the sore is gone

Add a pinch of turmeric for added antibacterial and anti-inflammatory effects.

Ghee contains butyric acid, a fatty acid with anti-inflammatory effects, which can therefore help to reduce any swelling and pain from the sores.

Coconut oil has antimicrobial properties, due to the presence of medium-chain fatty acids like lauric acid, and can therefore help kill bacteria which might be causing the sores.

Skin

Skin Remedies

PAGE 64 Acne & Breakouts

PAGE 74 Burns

PAGE 79 Corns & Calluses

PAGE 81 Cuts & Bruises

PAGE 85 Chapped or Dry Lips

PAGE 90 Dark Circles & Puffy Eyes

PAGE 93 Dry Skin

PAGE 97 Enlarged Pores

PAGE 100 Redness & Inflammation

PAGE 105 Scars & Hyperpigmentation

Acne & Breakouts

To improve the effectiveness of face masks, it's recommended to steam your face (see below) before applying the mask. You can also mix-and-match any of the ingredients in these remedies to make your own face masks; for example, you could mix together sandalwood, neem and rosewater, or mix together turmeric and honey.

Facial Steaming

2-4 cups water
1 bowl
1 towel

1 Bring the water to a boil or to the point of steaming in a kettle.

2 Pour the water into a bowl and place it on a table.

3 Sit down and hold your face above the bowl. Drape the towel over your head and the bowl to trap the steam.

NOTE

Don't put your face too close to the steam to avoid burning. Raise or lower your head for more or less heat and lift the towel to cool off if needed.

4 Steam your face for 5-10 minutes.

CAUTION

Do not do this if you suffer from rosacea

FREQUENCY

Once a week

ACNE & BREAKOUTS

You can add some herbs or oils to the bowl of hot water, such as chamomile, orange peel or lavender oil, for potential extra benefits.

> Steaming dilates the pores and can help to soften and loosen any sebum, dead skin cells, bacteria, and other impurities that can clog the pores and cause breakouts. This makes it easier for the impurities to be extracted from the pores. Steam also increases the skin's permeability, enabling it to better absorb acne-fighting ingredients applied afterwards, which could improve their effectiveness.

Turmeric Face Mask

1-2 tbsp gram flour
(you can also use whole-wheat flour)
1 tsp ground turmeric
2 tbsp probiotic/live yoghurt
2 tsp rosewater (optional)
1 tsp sandalwood powder OR
8-10 drops sandalwood oil (optional)

1. Mix together the ingredients in a bowl to create a thick paste. If it seems too dry, add more yoghurt or rosewater. If it seems too runny, add more of the turmeric or flour.
2. Apply to the skin and leave for 15-20 minutes.
3. Gently rub the mask on your skin as you wash it off to help exfoliate. Use a gentle cleanser to help remove the yellowish tint from your skin.

FREQUENCY

1-2 times a week

Gram flour is rich in zinc, which has been found to decrease sebum production and fight acne-causing bacteria including *P. acnes*. The fine, grainy texture of gram flour also makes it a mechanical exfoliant, helping to scrub away dead skin cells so they don't clog pores and cause breakouts.

Turmeric contains curcumin – a potent anti-inflammatory, antibacterial compound, and has been shown to inhibit growth of *P. acnes* as well as *S. aureus* – bacteria linked to acne. Turmeric's anti-inflammatory properties can also help to reduce swollen or inflamed pimples.

Yoghurt contains a small amount of lactic acid, which can gently exfoliate dead skin cells and sebum that might clog pores. Yoghurt simultaneously moisturises the skin, as lactic acid's structure allows it to bind water within the skin. Live yoghurt also contains probiotics, which have been shown to inhibit the growth of acne-causing bacteria such as *P. acnes*, as well as repairing the skin barrier, which reduces the ability of bacteria to penetrate the skin.

Rose water is antibacterial and anti-inflammatory, and it contains rose oil, which has been shown to combat various acne-causing bacteria. Rose water also acts as an astringent, which is commonly used to cleanse skin, remove excess oil and tighten pores, which can help to prevent future breakouts.

Sandalwood has notable anti-inflammatory effects on the skin, and has been found to combat numerous skin bacteria and fungi. Also, a clinical trial combining sandalwood with a small amount of salicylic acid found a significant improvement in those with mild to moderate acne.

Papaya & Sandalwood Mask

½ papaya
10-20 drops sandalwood oil (for all skin types) OR
2 tsp sandalwood powder (for oily skin)
1 tsp honey (optional)

1. Mash the papaya and mix it with the sandalwood to create a paste-like consistency. If it's too dry, you can add some water, rose water or more honey.
2. Apply to face and leave for 20 minutes.
3. Wash off with warm water.

FREQUENCY

1-2 times a week

Papaya contains enzymes such as papain, which is found in many exfoliating products, and can help to reduce acne by removing dead skin cells that may clog pores. Papain can also remove the damaged keratin that can build up on the skin and cause small bumps. Papaya's enzymes and phytochemicals also have antibacterial and anti-inflammatory properties which can further help to reduce breakouts and acne.

Sandalwood has notable anti-inflammatory effects on the skin, and has been found to combat numerous skin bacteria and fungi. Also, a clinical trial combining sandalwood with a small amount of salicylic acid found a significant improvement in those with mild to moderate acne.

Neem Spot Treatment

Neem oil OR a few neem leaves
OR ½-1 tsp neem leaf powder

If using neem oil:

1. Apply some neem oil on the affected area(s) using a cotton swab, cotton ball or clean fingers.
2. Leave for 20 minutes, then wash off with warm water.

If using neem leaves:

1. Blend the neem leaves with some water to get a paste-like consistency.
2. Apply the paste to the affected area(s).
3. Leave for 20 minutes, then wash off with warm water.

If using neem powder:

1. Mix the neem powder with some water to get a paste-like consistency.
2. Apply the paste to the affected area(s).
3. Leave for 20 minutes, then wash off with warm water.

FREQUENCY

Use daily until you get the desired result

Neem contains antibacterial, antifungal, antiseptic and anti-inflammatory compounds, all of which are helpful properties for reducing and preventing breakouts. Neem has been found to effectively fight several strains of bacteria, including *S. aureus* – a bacterium linked to acne. Neem is also rich in essential fatty acids and vitamin E, which help to moisturise dry skin; this is important as dry skin can result in increased sebum production, which can then build up and cause breakouts.

Neem Toner

½ handful neem leaves OR 1 tsp neem powder
1 cup water

1. Bring the water to a boil in a pan, then remove from heat.
2. Mix in the neem leaves or powder and leave for 20 minutes.
3. Strain out the leaves (if you used powder, no need to strain as it will have dissolved) and leave to cool completely.
4. Apply the neem water to your face as a toner using a cotton pad or spray bottle.

FREQUENCY

1-2 times a day

NOTE

Store any remaining toner in the fridge for up to 2 weeks.

You can adjust the concentration of the toner by steeping the neem leaves for more or less time, or using more or less of the powder in the water.

Cinnamon & Honey Spot Treatment

2 tsp honey
½ tsp ground cinnamon

1. Mix the honey and cinnamon to create a paste.
2. Cleanse your face, then apply the paste to the affected area(s).
3. Leave for 15-30 minutes then wash off.

FREQUENCY

Use daily till you get the desired result

This can also be used as a face mask. Simply make more of the mixture to cover your whole face.

Honey and cinnamon are both well-documented to combat bacteria and inflammation – two factors that trigger acne. Research has found that the combination of honey and cinnamon exerted antibacterial effects against *P. acnes*. Cinnamon is also a mild astringent due to the tannins it contains, which is often used to remove excess oil and tighten pores, helping to reduce future breakouts.

Aloe Vera & Green Tea Moisturiser

4 tsp fresh aloe vera gel OR store-bought organic aloe vera gel
Green tea bag OR leaves
½ cup water
4 drops of your choice of oil e.g. rosehip, tea tree, lavender, sweet almond oil (optional)

1 Brew the green tea in half a cup of water and let it cool in a bowl or container.

2 Mix together the aloe vera, 2 teaspoons of the brewed green tea (the liquid not the leaves) and oil (if using).

3 Apply this to your face as a moisturiser.

FREQUENCY

Once or twice daily (morning and night or just at night)

NOTE

Store in an airtight container in the fridge for up to 3 days.

You can also make this into a toner by just adding more brewed green tea (the liquid) to make a runnier consistency.

Green tea contains a number of polyphenols, and is especially rich in EGCG, which research has shown to have anti-inflammatory, antioxidant and antimicrobial properties, and inhibit the growth of acne-causing bacteria (*P. acnes*). EGCG is also anti-androgenic (androgens are hormones that when high or fluctuating, stimulate more sebum production, causing hormonal acne). These properties are likely why green tea has been found to reduce pimples, acne severity and sebum production when applied to the skin.

Aloe vera has powerful anti-inflammatory properties as well, and it contains salicylic acid and sulphur – both of which are used extensively to treat acne. Aloe vera is also antibacterial, due to the presence of compounds called anthraquinones, and so can help to combat bacteria that might be causing acne and breakouts. Aloe vera is also very hydrating, which helps to moisturise dry skin, preventing increased sebum production and the resulting clogged pores.

Garlic Spot Treatment

1 garlic clove, peeled

1 Cut one end off the clove and slash some small lines on this end so that the juice can easily transfer to your skin.
2 Rub the cut end of the clove on the pimple(s) so that they are lightly coated in garlic juice.
3 Leave overnight and wash your face in the morning.

If you have sensitive skin, you can mince the garlic clove and mix it with 1 tbsp water or rose water. Apply this to the affected areas for 5-10 minutes, then wash it off.

Garlic can help reduce breakouts as it is known to have antibacterial, antifungal and antiseptic properties, with a recent study finding that garlic juice helps to fight *P. acnes* – an acne-causing bacteria. Garlic also reduces swelling and inflammation, and improves blood circulation in the skin, therefore helping to deliver more oxygen and nutrients to the skin. Garlic also contains several vitamins and minerals believed to combat acne, including zinc and vitamin C.

Cumin, Coriander & Fennel Tea

Cumin seeds
Coriander seeds
Fennel seeds
Water

1. Combine equal parts of all the seeds and store in a glass jar in a cupboard.
2. Add 1 teaspoon of the seed mix to a mug of boiling water.
3. Let it brew for 5-10 minutes, then strain out the seeds and drink.

FREQUENCY

1-2 times a day

You can add a little cinnamon or honey to sweeten the taste if needed.

NOTE

The seed mix will last for 1-3 years. To check if it's still good to use, crush each type of seed and check they still have a fragrance. If it doesn't smell like much, it won't make you ill, but it may have lost its potency and associated benefits.

Both cumin and coriander have been found to regulate blood sugar, which is important as certain foods can raise blood sugar quickly, causing the body to release insulin; insulin makes androgen hormones more active, which can cause increased sebum production and therefore increase the risk of acne. Furthermore, all three seeds contain powerful antioxidants, including vitamin C and quercetin, as well as nutrients crucial for the skin and immune health like vitamins A, D and E and zinc, all of which have also been found to reduce inflammation.

Burns

These remedies can be used for first and second-degree burns, including sunburn. If the burn is more serious, for example if it has pus or open sores, the pain is severe, or you get a fever, please seek medical treatment.

Aloe Vera Moisturiser

2 tbsp fresh aloe vera gel
OR store-bought organic aloe vera gel
8-10 drops lavender oil (optional)
3-5 drops peppermint oil (optional)

1. Apply the aloe vera gel to the affected area(s) in place of your moisturiser. If using fresh aloe, make sure you're not applying any of the yellow juice (aloe latex).
2. Leave to dry.

FREQUENCY

Daily, as many times as needed

NOTE

If using just lavender oil, use 15 drops and if using just peppermint oil, use 10 drops.

Put in the fridge before use for a more soothing, cooling sensation.

Research shows that aloe vera is effective at treating first and second-degree burns. Aloe vera has cooling and moisturising effects, which help to soothe the burn, hydrate the dried, burned skin and prevent the peeling that sometimes occurs. It also has anti-inflammatory and antibacterial properties, due to the presence of aloin and anthraquinones, which help to reduce swelling and prevent infections from the burn.

Lavender oil has been found to promote the healing of wounds, including burns, as well as having pain-relieving and anti-inflammatory properties, due to the presence of compounds like beta-caryophyllene and linalyl acetate.

Peppermint oil is rich in menthol, which has a cooling effect on the burn. It also has analgesic and anti-inflammatory properties, which can help to reduce the pain and swelling that might accompany the burn.

Cucumber & Rose Water

1 small cucumber OR ½ large cucumber, peeled and chopped
Water
2-3 tsp rose water

1. Add the cucumber to a pan with enough water to cover all the pieces.
2. Heat on a low flame for 5-10 minutes.
3. Transfer the contents to a blender or food processer and blend until smooth.
4. Strain the liquid into a spray bottle or container and add in the rose water.
5. Spray or apply to face whenever you need relief or as a toner.

FREQUENCY

As often as needed

NOTE

Store in the fridge for up to 4 days.

You can soak the cucumber pieces in a pan of brewed green tea instead of plain water for added benefits.

Cucumber is highly hydrating as it is around 95% water, which helps to moisturise and soothe the dry, burned skin. Cucumbers also contain several antioxidants, such as vitamin C and caffeic acid, which help to reduce inflammation and can also neutralise the increased free radicals that often cause scarring.

Rose water has been found to soothe the skin and reduce redness due to its anti-inflammatory effects, especially for inflammation caused by UV exposure. Rose water also has antibacterial, antiseptic and analgesic properties, meaning that it can help to treat and prevent infections that could result from burns, as well as providing pain relief.

Camphor, Sesame Oil & Honey

If using on your face for sunburn, then only leave the mixture on for 20-30 minutes before washing off.

10 drops camphor oil
1 tbsp sesame oil
(refined sesame oil if using on face)
1 tbsp honey

1. Mix together the sesame oil, camphor oil and honey.
2. You can add more honey if it's too runny.
3. Apply the mixture to the burn or affected area(s).
4. Place a dressing on the burn if needed.
5. Leave on for as long as you like (at least 20-30 minutes), then wash off any residue. Change the dressing more frequently than this if it becomes saturated.

FREQUENCY

Daily or as often as needed

SHORTCUT

You can just apply sesame oil or honey by itself as they are individually effective for burns as well.

NOTE

If you only have camphor blocks or tablets, you can melt half of one in the sesame oil, but wait for the mixture to cool before applying it.

Honey has been shown to significantly reduce the healing time of superficial and partial thickness burns when compared with conventional dressings. This could be because of honey's anti-inflammatory properties and acidic pH, which reduces the presence of proteases (substances that impair healing) and encourages the blood to release oxygen (important for wound healing). Honey also has an antimicrobial effect on bacteria commonly present in wounds and burns.

Sesame oil has been found to accelerate the healing process for burns, due to its anti-inflammatory, antimicrobial and antioxidant properties. Sesame oil also contains several essential fatty acids, which help to moisturise dried, burned skin and relieve itchiness.

Camphor has been found to heal partial thickness or second-degree burns quicker when mixed with sesame oil and honey. Like sesame oil and honey, camphor has anti-inflammatory and antibacterial properties, but also provides pain relief when applied topically, which is why it's used as an analgesic in a number of lotions and balms.

Corns & Calluses

The following remedies are described assuming foot calluses, but can be used for hands too.

Castor Oil Soak

5 tbsp castor oil
1 large container, bowl or tub (big enough to fit both feet)
Water

1. Fill the container with enough warm water to cover your feet up to the ankles.
2. Add the castor oil to the water.
3. Soak your feet in this for about 20 minutes.
4. Use a pumice stone or foot file to rub the callus in circular or side-to-side motions, applying gentle pressure.

FREQUENCY

As needed, up to 2-3 times a week

NOTE

Don't try to remove the whole callus in one go – the idea is to use this remedy over a period of time to gradually remove the dead skin.

> The warm water softens the corn and calluses and loosens some of the dead skin. Castor oil is rich in monounsaturated fatty acids like ricinoleic acid, which act as humectants to moisturise and soften the skin. This helps to soften the corns and calluses, making it easier to file off the dead skin with the pumice stone or foot file.

Buttermilk & Honey Foot Mask

2 tbsp buttermilk (can be substituted for almond milk but won't be as exfoliating)
2 tbsp honey
1 pair socks

1. Warm the buttermilk and honey in the microwave, then mix to create a paste. You can add more honey or buttermilk as needed to achieve the right consistency.
2. Apply the mixture to your feet, focusing on the dry, calloused areas.
3. Put on socks and leave overnight.
4. Rinse in the morning with warm water or in the shower.

FREQUENCY

Daily or as often as needed

You can make a larger quantity and store in a jar in the fridge to use within 1-2 weeks. Make sure to warm it slightly before use.

Buttermilk contains lactic acid – a chemical exfoliant – which helps to loosen the bonds between dead skin cells, allowing them to be gently removed, leaving behind softer skin. Lactic acid, unlike other chemical exfoliants, also helps to improve the skin's natural moisture factor because its structure allows it to bind water within skin.

Honey helps to moisturise and soften the hard, dry skin as it is a humectant, so it helps to seal in moisture in the skin. Honey also has antimicrobial properties, which can help prevent infections that could result from cracked skin on the feet.

Cuts & Bruises

Turmeric, Garlic & Coconut Oil Paste

1 tsp turmeric
1 garlic clove, crushed
2 tsp coconut oil
½ inch fresh ginger, grated (optional)

1 Melt the coconut oil in a small bowl in the microwave. Do this in 10 second intervals, as the oil melts quite quickly.

2 Add the turmeric, garlic and ginger (if using) to the bowl of melted coconut oil.

3 Stir all the ingredients together to make a paste-like consistency.

4 Apply directly to the affected area and cover with a bandage if needed.

5 Leave for 30 minutes then wash off with water.

FREQUENCY

Up to 3 times a day

FOR A FRESH BRUISE

Apply ice or a cold compress over the bandage to reduce the amount of blood that leaks into the surrounding area.

FOR 1-2 DAYS AFTER THE BRUISE

Apply a warm compress over the bandage to help dilate the surrounding blood vessels and increase blood flow, allowing the leaked blood to be reabsorbed more quickly.

Turmeric contains curcumin, which has potent anti-inflammatory and antimicrobial properties, and can therefore protect against infections and reduce swelling from cuts and bruises. Turmeric has also been found to speed up several stages of the wound healing process, such as wound contraction and new tissue formation.

Garlic contains allicin, which has anti-inflammatory and antimicrobial properties, and so can help to reduce swelling from cuts or bruises and prevent infections. Garlic has also been shown to speed up healing by increasing the number of proliferating fibroblasts – these are essential in healing cuts and bruises as they stimulate the growth of new tissue and blood vessels.

Coconut oil is high in various fatty acids which help to protect cuts from getting infected due to their antimicrobial effects. Coconut oil also has anti-inflammatory and analgesic properties, which can reduce swelling and pain caused by cuts or bruises. Coconut oil, like garlic, has been shown to speed up healing by increasing fibroblast proliferation.

Ginger contains gingerol, which has been found to promote new blood vessel formation after a cut or bruise and increase blood flow in the repairing tissue, which helps to deliver sufficient oxygen and nutrients and clear away leaked blood. Also, ginger and turmeric have been found to have complementary effects when used together for wound healing.

Pineapple

Pineapple is effective for bruising both when applied topically or consumed. If using for a cut, it should only be consumed. The pineapple can be used in the following ways:

- Slice the pineapple and apply a slice to the bruise for about 20 minutes. Repeat this about 3 times a day. DO NOT use this method for cuts.
- Consume 1-2 cups of pineapple daily, whether you eat it, juice it, or add it to a smoothie. Do this until the bruise has faded or cut has healed.

If you often bruise or get cuts easily, consume about 1 cup of pineapple every day.

Pineapple contains bromelain – a mixture of enzymes found to significantly reduce inflammation, and the duration and severity of a bruise. Pineapple is also rich in vitamin C, with one cup containing more than 100% of the recommended daily intake. Vitamin C is essential for collagen production, which helps to strengthen skin and blood vessels for those prone to regular cuts and bruises, as well as speeding up healing by stimulating growth of new tissue and blood vessels.

Onion & Honey Paste

¼–½ onion, roughly chopped
Honey

1. Crush the raw onion using a blender or mixer. Add a small amount of water if needed.
2. Mix the crushed onion with enough honey to make a paste.
3. Apply directly to the affected area and cover with a cloth or bandage.
4. Leave for 20-30 minutes then wash off with water.

FREQUENCY

Up to 3 times a day

Onion contains quercetin, which is used in various creams and gels that help with bruising, likely due to the compound's anti-inflammatory effect. Onions also have antibacterial properties, due to compounds like quercetin and allicin, which can help protect cuts from getting infected.

Honey has been shown to fight bacteria commonly present in cuts and wounds, and can therefore help prevent an infection. The sugar present in honey also keeps bacterial cells from multiplying as it draws water out of these cells. The sugar also helps to draw water out of damaged tissues, which can reduce the swelling of cuts and bruises. Honey can also speed up the healing process as its acidic pH reduces the presence of proteases – substances that impair healing.

Aloe Vera Gel

Fresh aloe vera gel OR
store-bought organic aloe vera gel

Apply the aloe vera gel to the cut or bruised area. There is no need to wash this off the skin – simply leave it on until it's soaked in and reapply as needed.

FREQUENCY

As often as needed

You can mix the aloe vera with other ingredients in this section, such as honey or turmeric, for added benefits. If you do mix it with other ingredients, make sure to wash off the mixture after 30 minutes.

Aloe vera has been found to speed up the healing of cuts and bruises, partly because it contains a compound called glucomannan, which promotes cellular regeneration and collagen production. Aloe vera can also help prevent the cut from getting infected, as it has antimicrobial properties due to the presence of compounds like anthraquinones. Aloe vera's anti-inflammatory and analgesic properties can help reduce pain and swelling caused by the bruise.

Chapped or Dry Lips

Start by exfoliating your lips, then moisturise and soothe with the honey and avocado lip mask, and finish with aloe vera or a lip balm.

Sugar & Ghee Scrub

1 tsp ghee OR coconut oil, melted
1 tsp brown OR caster sugar
¼-½ tsp ground cinnamon (optional for if you want to plump and bring colour to your lips)

1. Combine all the ingredients in a small bowl to make the scrub.
2. Using your finger, apply the scrub to your lips and gently scrub in a circular motion for about 30-60 seconds.
3. Rinse off the scrub with warm water and gently pat dry.
4. Apply a lip balm or use a moisturising lip mask (see page 87).

FREQUENCY

2-3 times a week

NOTE

The cinnamon may sting or tingle a little but don't worry – this is normal.

Store any remaining scrub in a small container in a cool, dry location.

> Ghee, like coconut oil, contains several fatty acids, including oleic acid, which are easily absorbed and moisturise the lips. A lack of fatty acids in the epithelial tissue can often cause lip chapping, so ghee helps to restore this. Ghee is also rich in vitamin E – a well-known moisturising agent – which relieves dry lips by promoting cell turnover and bringing new cells to the surface faster.

Sugar is the exfoliant that makes this a scrub – the granules buff away the dead skin cells, and allow the lips to better absorb moisturising agents.

Cinnamon contains cassia oil, which is calming when applied to skin, but irritates the mucus membrane on the lips. As a result, the blood circulation to the lips increases, which plumps them and adds some colour.

Papaya Exfoliator

This is a gentler alternative to a lip scrub.

2-3 cubes papaya

1. Mash the papaya cubes.
2. Apply to lips and leave on for 15-30 minutes.
3. Rinse off lips with warm water and gently pat dry.
4. Apply a lip balm or use a moisturising lip mask (see next page).

FREQUENCY

2-3 times a week

Papaya contains enzymes like papain and AHAs like glycolic acid, which both help to remove dead skin and regenerate new cells. It is also rich in antioxidants like vitamin C and lycopene, which can protect the lips against environmental damage like sun exposure, which often dries out lips. Papaya's high moisture content (over 80% water) helps to hydrate the lips.

Honey & Avocado Lip Mask

1 tsp honey
2 tsp mashed avocado

1 Mix together the honey and avocado.
2 Apply the mixture to your lips and leave on for 15-30 minutes.
3 Rinse lips with warm water and gently pat dry.

CAUTION

Do not do this if you have a latex-fruit allergy

FREQUENCY

2-3 times a week

Honey can moisturise dry lips as it is a humectant, meaning it draws water into the top layer of the skin. Honey can also protect cracked lips from infection due to its antimicrobial properties.

Avocado is an effective emollient for lips due to the several fatty acids it contains, like oleic acid, which moisturise the lips and have been found to speed up healing. Avocado is also rich in vitamin E, which relieves dry lips by promoting cell turnover and bringing new cells to the surface faster. Vitamin E is an antioxidant as well, therefore helping to protect against environmental damage like sun exposure, which often dries out lips.

Aloe Vera Gel

1 tsp fresh aloe vera gel OR store-bought organic aloe vera gel
½ tsp coconut oil (optional)

1 Mix the fresh aloe vera gel with the coconut oil (if using, make sure it's softened first).

2 Apply to lips both morning and night and whenever needed during the day.

FREQUENCY

Daily

NOTE

Whilst fresh aloe vera gel can be tricky to apply on the go, if you are using store-bought aloe vera, then you can apply it instead of lip balm during the day.

The polysaccharides in aloe vera bind moisture to the skin, helping the lips feel less dry. These polysaccharides, along with growth hormones (gibberellins and auxins), stimulate the skin to produce new cells to replace the dead skin. Aloe vera's anti-inflammatory properties can help fight irritation and inflammation – a common cause of chapped lips, and its antioxidants help protect the lips from environmental damage.

Coconut oil is an effective occlusive and emollient due to its fatty acid content, meaning it forms a protective film on the lips which helps to shield them from environmental damage, and keeps lips soft by stopping moisture from escaping. It can also help the aloe vera stay on the lips during the day, because aloe by itself is absorbed quickly.

Ghee & Honey Lip Balm

5 tsp ghee, melted
1 tsp honey
1 small container

1. Mix together the melted ghee and honey.
2. Pour into a small container and leave to solidify (it will solidify at room temperature but you can put it in the fridge to speed up the process).
3. Apply to lips with your finger.

FREQUENCY

As often as needed

Ghee contains several fatty acids, including oleic acid, which are easily absorbed and moisturise the lips. A lack of fatty acids in the epithelial tissue can often cause lip chapping, so ghee helps to restore this. Ghee is also rich in vitamin E – a well-known moisturising agent – which relieves dry lips by promoting cell turnover and bringing new cells to the surface faster.

Honey can help moisturise dry lips as it is a humectant, meaning it draws water into the top layer of the skin. Honey can also protect cracked lips from infection due to its antimicrobial properties.

Dark Cirles & Puffy Eyes

Note that dark circles and puffiness can be hereditary, so whilst the following remedies may work for dark circles and puffiness caused by a number of factors, it's possible they may not help if the cause is genetic.

Turmeric Buttermilk Eye Mask

1 tbsp ground turmeric
1 tbsp buttermilk

1 Mix the turmeric and buttermilk together in a small bowl.

2 Apply this mixture to the under-eye area – it might help to apply it if you use a small brush. Be careful not to get it in your eyes.

3 Let the mixture dry on your skin for about 15 minutes.

4 Wash off with water or a wet cloth.

FREQUENCY

Up to a few times a week

Turmeric temporarily stains the skin yellow, which effectively acts as a colour corrector for the dark, purplish colour under the eyes. Research has also shown turmeric to reduce hyperpigmentation, and so can brighten the under eye area. Turmeric's powerful antioxidant properties – due to the presence of curcumin – also helps to prevent possible causes of dark circles, such as UV damage from the sun. Meanwhile, curcumin's anti-inflammatory properties can help reduce puffiness resulting from factors like allergies.

Buttermilk has astringent properties, meaning it can help reduce puffiness by pulling the skin taut. It also contains lactic acid, which gently exfoliates dead skin cells whilst moisturising too, as its structure allows it to bind water within the skin. Exfoliation encourages collagen production and new cell growth, which helps to thicken the thin skin under the eyes, reducing how visible the dark, underlying veins are.

Chilled Potato Patches

1 potato

1. Put a washed potato in the fridge overnight.
2. Cut two slices of the potato in the morning. Put the rest of the potato back in the fridge in an airtight container.
3. Apply the slices on closed eyes for 10-15 minutes. If the slices get warm before the time is up, just cut two new slices.

FREQUENCY

As often as needed

Potatoes contain vitamin C and niacin, both of which have been shown to be effective skin-brightening agents; they can reduce and prevent dark circles caused by hyperpigmentation by diminishing melanin production and its transfer to the top layer of the skin. Meanwhile, the coldness of the potato slices can combat puffiness by reducing swelling and shrinking blood vessels, which also minimises darkness.

Castor & Almond Oil

2 drops castor oil
2 drops sweet almond oil

1. Mix the castor and almond oil.
2. Apply to the under-eye area at night using your ring finger.
3. Wash off the next morning if there is anything left.

FREQUENCY

Every night

Castor oil has anti-inflammatory properties which can help reduce puffiness under the eyes. Castor oil can also stimulate the production of collagen and elastin. These proteins form the base of skin, and can help thicken the thin skin under the eyes, reducing the visibility of the underlying veins (a common cause of the appearance of dark circles).

Almond oil contains retinol, vitamin E and vitamin K. Retinol encourages the production of collagen and elastin, helping to thicken the under-eye skin. It also increases cell turnover, which speeds up the reduction of hyperpigmentation. Vitamin E reduces dark circles by inhibiting tyrosinase – the critical enzyme in the production of pigment. Vitamin K combined with retinol and vitamin E, has been shown to effectively reduce dark circles. Almond oil's anti-inflammatory and sclerosant (causes veins to contract and not be as visible) properties can help reduce puffiness.

Dry Skin

The following remedies are suitable for the face and body.

Banana Peel Mask

1 banana peel
2 tbsp honey
1 avocado (optional)

1. Blend the banana peel, honey and avocado (if using).
2. Apply the mixture to the affected area(s).
3. Leave for 20 minutes then wash it off.

CAUTION

Do not use if you have a latex-fruit allergy

FREQUENCY

Up to twice a day

SHORTCUT

You can just rub the banana peel on the affected area(s) for about 20 minutes or until the peel turns brown.

> Banana peels are abundant in fatty acids, such as palmitic, oleic and linoleic acids, which are known to replenish moisture in the skin and strengthen the skin barrier to prevent moisture loss. Banana peels are also rich in potassium – an electrolyte – which attracts water and can therefore help hydrate the skin. Research has found that applying a potassium compound can improve dry skin and eczema, likely due to these skin conditions being associated with depleted potassium in the skin's outer layer.

> Honey is an emollient and humectant, meaning it draws water into the top layer of the skin, helping to hydrate and soften dry skin. Honey has also been found to speed up the healing process of broken skin that might result from dry skin or eczema, and reduce any accompanying irritation and itching.

Jojoba, Turmeric & Neem Oil Mask

1 tsp jojoba OR sweet almond oil
1 tsp ground turmeric
10 drops neem oil OR 1 handful neem leaves OR ½-1 tsp neem leaf powder

If using neem oil or powder:

1. Mix together all the ingredients to make a paste. Add some water or more jojoba/sweet almond oil if needed.
2. Apply the paste to the affected area(s).
3. Leave for 20 minutes, then wash it off.

If using neem leaves:

1. Crush and grind the neem leaves.
2. Mix in the turmeric and oil to make a paste. Add more oil if needed.
3. Apply the paste to the affected area(s).
4. Leave for 20 minutes, then wash it off.

FREQUENCY

Up to twice a week

Research has shown jojoba oil to improve dry skin and related skin conditions, like eczema. The oil has a similar structure to the skin's own sebum, so it absorbs quickly and balances the skin's oils, adding moisture where needed without causing excess oil and breakouts. Jojoba oil is an emollient and occlusive due to its fatty acid content, meaning that it helps to soften the skin and prevent water loss. The vitamin E content also relieves dry skin by promoting cell turnover and bringing new cells to the surface faster, as well as helping to repair the skin barrier, which prevents moisture from escaping.

Neem oil has been found to be effective at reducing water loss from the skin. Neem oil is rich in fatty acids such as palmitic, oleic and linoleic acids, which replenish moisture in the skin and support the skin barrier to prevent moisture loss. Neem is also high in vitamin E which, as outlined previously, further helps to relieve dry skin.

Turmeric contains curcumin, which has potent anti-inflammatory and antioxidant properties. This helps to protect and fight damage caused to the skin barrier by free radicals, which in turn reduces water loss from the skin and prevents it from drying out as much. Turmeric has also been found to help alleviate conditions causing dry skin such as eczema.

Milk Cream (Malai) & Rose Water

5 cups unhomogenised whole milk
1 tsp rose water
1 large, wide-mouthed glass jar OR 1 saucepan

You can collect the cream in two different ways:

Method 1:

1 Pour the milk into the glass jar and leave to sit for 24 hours.

2 Find the line where the milk and cream separate – you should be able to tell as the cream will be thicker and less translucent than the milk. If you can't tell, you might need to leave it for longer to separate.

3 Scoop out the cream using a ladle or measuring cup and transfer to a bowl. Don't go too deep otherwise you'll pick up the milk.

4 Repeat until there is a thin line of cream left in the jar of milk.

Method 2:

1 Boil the milk in a pan for 10 minutes, stirring constantly.

2 Leave to cool in the pan, then put it in the refrigerator and leave overnight.

3 Remove the thick layer of cream that forms on top of the milk using a slotted spoon and transfer to a bowl or container.

Once you have collected the cream, mix it with rose water, apply to the dry skin for 20-30 minutes, then wash off.

FREQUENCY

Up to three times a week

NOTE

Any leftover cream can be stored in the fridge for up to 5 days.

Milk cream (or malai) is mostly made up of fat and protein, and contains multiple fatty acids, including oleic acid, which moisturise the skin. Milk and its proteins have been found to have anti-inflammatory effects, which can help relieve itching caused by dry skin as well as inflammatory skin conditions like eczema.

Rose water's low pH helps to restore the skin's natural pH, which can soothe and hydrate dry skin, as an off-balance skin pH can cause dry skin. Skin conditions like eczema and psoriasis, which often cause dry skin, have also been associated with a disturbed skin pH. Rose water also has antioxidant properties, so it can limit free radicals that cause skin barrier damage and water loss.

Enlarged Pores

Before using any of these masks, it may help to steam your face or the area with enlarged pores. This can help to loosen any impurities that may be trapped in the pores and causing the larger appearance, so that these impurities can be more easily targeted by the masks.

Cinnamon & Honey Mask

½ tsp ground cinnamon OR 5 drops cinnamon oil
2 tsp honey
½ tsp ground nutmeg (optional)

1. Mix together the cinnamon, honey and nutmeg (if using) to make a paste.
2. Apply to the area(s) with enlarged pores.
3. Leave for 10 minutes.
4. Gently wash off whilst rubbing in circular motions.

FREQUENCY

Up to twice a week

Cinnamon is a mild astringent due to the tannins it contains, which helps to remove excess oil and dirt that might have settled into the pores and made them appear larger. Cinnamon is also loaded with powerful antioxidants, and can therefore protect against free radicals that reduce collagen and elastin – the depletion of which is a major cause of enlarged pores. Meanwhile, the cinnamaldehyde in cinnamon has been found to promote collagen production, which can further improve the skin's elasticity and reduce pore size.

Honey's antimicrobial properties can help to kill bacteria that may be clogging pores and causing their larger appearance. Honey also acts as a humectant, drawing moisture to the skin. This is important as the skin shouldn't be left dry or stripped of moisture, as more sebum may then be produced, which could collect in the pores and make them appear larger.

Nutmeg has a grainy texture that works as a gentle exfoliator, and so can help to remove trapped impurities that often make pores look bigger, like dead skin cells and excess sebum. Nutmeg has also been found to combat a reduction in collagen caused by sun exposure, due to its antioxidant properties.

Sandalwood & Rosewater Mask

1 tsp sandalwood powder
1-2 tsp rose water

1. Mix together the sandalwood powder and rose water to make a thin paste.
2. Apply this paste on the area(s) with enlarged pores.
3. Leave for 10-20 minutes.
4. Wash off, then apply your usual moisturiser or your usual skincare routine.

FREQUENCY

Up to twice a week

Sandalwood is a mild astringent, meaning it can help to remove excess oil or sebum – a common cause of pores looking enlarged as the sebum can clog up and 'stretch' the pore opening. Astringents also help to constrict soft tissue, therefore tightening the skin and reducing the appearance of large pores.

Rose water is an astringent and antibacterial as well, and its rose oil content has been shown to combat bacteria, such as *P. acnes*, which can thrive in clogged pores, causing additional issues such as acne or breakouts.

Frothy Egg White Mask

1 egg

1. Separate the egg white from the yolk into a bowl.
2. Beat the egg white until slightly stiff and foamy.
3. Apply this on the area(s) with enlarged pores.
4. Leave for 10 minutes.
5. Wash off, then apply your usual moisturiser or your usual skincare routine.

FREQUENCY

No more than once a week

NOTE

This will only provide a temporary pore-tightening effect.

Egg whites are rich in proteins, and have been found to reduce excess oil and tighten skin. These proteins, such as ovalbumin, also function as humectants, which help to draw moisture to the skin, temporarily plumping and tightening the skin. Egg whites also contain proline and glycine – amino acids that are essential for collagen production and can therefore firm the skin, reducing the appearance of large pores.

Redness & Inflamation

Oat & Turmeric Mask

½ cup colloidal oatmeal OR oatmeal flakes
½ cup warm water
1-2 tsp ground turmeric

NOTE

If you are using oatmeal flakes, grind them into a fine powder before using to make it into colloidal oatmeal.

1. Mix together the oatmeal, turmeric and water to make a paste.
2. Apply the paste to the red, inflamed area(s).
3. Leave for 15 minutes.
4. Gently wash off with warm water.

FREQUENCY

Up to twice a week

To test if the oatmeal flakes are ground fine enough, add some to a cup of warm water – the water should absorb it and turn milky.

Colloidal oatmeal contains compounds called avenanthramides, as well as vitamin E and ferulic acid, all of which have exhibited anti-inflammatory and anti-itch properties for the skin, and can therefore calm inflammation and the associated redness. Colloidal oatmeal also contains starches, beta-glucan, water-binding polysaccharides and hydrocolloids, which help to repair the moisture barrier and protect the skin from external irritants that may be causing redness and inflammation.

Turmeric, like oatmeal, also has powerful anti-inflammatory and antioxidant properties due to its compound curcumin. Antioxidants are helpful in preventing inflammation in the first place, as they can protect against free radicals that damage the skin and cause inflammation and irritation. Turmeric can also temporarily stain the skin slightly yellow, which colour corrects any red or pink tones.

Fenugreek Seed Mask

1 tbsp fenugreek seeds (adjust the quantity based on how much skin you are applying it to)
2 tbsp warm water
Blender

1. Soak the fenugreek seeds overnight in a bowl with the warm water.
2. Blend the seeds along with the water they soaked in (note that this will be slimy) to make a thick paste. Add more water if needed.
3. Apply the paste to the red, inflamed area(s). You may need to pat or press it into the skin to keep it in place.
4. Leave for 15-30 minutes.
5. Wash off with warm water, then apply your usual moisturiser.

FREQUENCY

Up to three times a week

NOTE

If you can only find fenugreek powder, then mix a spoonful of this with some water, rose water or aloe vera to make a paste, and apply as normal.

> Fenugreek seeds have anti-inflammatory properties due to their high antioxidant content, and can therefore reduce skin inflammation. Fenugreek seeds also have emollient properties, and have been found to soothe skin and improve its moisture content due to the seeds' mucilage content. This helps the skin retain water, reducing the ability of irritants to penetrate the skin and cause inflammation and redness.

Liquorice & Green Tea Toner

2 liquorice root sticks OR 1 tsp liquorice root powder
1 tsp green tea leaves OR green tea bag
1 cup water

If using liquorice sticks:

1. Bring the water to a boil in a pan and add the liquorice sticks.
2. Simmer on low heat for 5 minutes, then remove from heat.
3. Add the green tea to the water and leave for 20 minutes.
4. Strain the liquid into a spray bottle or container and refrigerate.
5. Apply to clean skin using the spray bottle or a cotton pad.
6. Follow with moisturiser or your usual skincare routine.

If using liquorice powder:

1. Boil the water and pour into a pan or bowl.
2. Add the green tea and brew for 5-10 minutes.
3. Mix in the liquorice powder and keep stirring until dissolved.
4. Strain the mixture into a spray bottle or container and refrigerate.
5. Apply to clean skin using the spray bottle or a cotton pad.
6. Follow with moisturiser or your usual skincare routine.

FREQUENCY

Up to twice a day

NOTE

Store in the fridge and use within 3-4 days.

You can also use this liquorice and green tea infused water as an addition or in place of normal water to any DIY face masks you use.

Liquorice contains glycyrrhizin – an anti-inflammatory compound which has been found to relieve red, irritated skin. Liquorice also contains glabridin, a component with antioxidant and skin-soothing properties, and can therefore help to protect against free radicals that damage the skin and cause inflammation, whilst being suitable for sensitive skin.

Green tea is anti-inflammatory due to its high content of polyphenols and catechins such as EGCG, and has been found to reduce skin irritation and redness, including that caused by conditions like rosacea, dermatitis and psoriasis. EGCG's potent antioxidant properties have also been found to help repair damage caused by UV exposure from the sun, which is a common trigger of redness and inflammation.

Aloe & Rose Moisturiser

4 tsp fresh aloe vera gel OR store-bought organic aloe vera gel
2 tsp rose water (optional)

1 Mix together the gel and rose water (if using).

2 Apply this gel mixture to red, inflamed area(s) as a moisturiser.

FREQUENCY

Up to twice a day

You can also use this as a toner by adding some more rose water and applying using a spray bottle or cotton pad.

Aloe vera has powerful anti-inflammatory and antioxidant properties, which have been shown to reduce skin inflammation and protect against free radicals that may cause irritation. Aloe vera has been found particularly effective at reducing redness caused by UV exposure. Aloe vera can also help to soothe inflamed skin due to its cooling effect when applied, and moisturises skin without leaving any residue that might irritate skin like some heavier creams do.

Rose water, like aloe vera, has strong anti-inflammatory, antioxidant and skin-soothing properties which can reduce redness and inflammation. Rose water's naturally low pH can help to balance the skin's pH level; this is important as redness, irritation and inflammation can be signs of the skin pH being too high.

Scars & Hyperpigmentation

Orange Peel Mask

2 tsp orange peel powder
1-2 tsp probiotic/live yoghurt OR honey

1 Mix all the ingredients together to make a paste. You can make more or less of the mixture depending on how much skin you need to cover.

2 Apply to the affected area(s) of skin.

3 Leave for 20 minutes, then wash off thoroughly.

FREQUENCY

Up to three times a week

NOTE

Apply sun screen during the day as this mask can increase photosensitivity.

You can make your own orange peel powder by peeling a few oranges, letting the peels dry out over a few days and then blending into a powder. You can also dry the peels in the oven for a quicker option, but keep an eye on them as they burn easily.

Orange peel powder contains hesperidin and vitamin C, both of which are potent antioxidants with skin-lightening effects by suppressing the production of melanin (the overproduction of melanin is what causes hyperpigmentation). Vitamin C can also help to heal atrophic scars – scars that look like indentations – by increasing the synthesis of collagen, therefore helping to rebuild healthy skin.

Yoghurt contains a low percentage of lactic acid, which gently exfoliates the skin, and has been shown to reduce superficial scarring and hyperpigmentation. Exfoliation also encourages collagen production and new cell growth, which could help to heal atrophic scarring.

Honey has been found to minimise hypertrophic scarring – scars that appear raised – from fresh wounds by keeping the area moist and promoting rapid healing.

Nutmeg & Turmeric Paste

1 tsp turmeric
1 tsp ground nutmeg
1 tbsp yoghurt OR honey
½ tsp sandalwood powder OR 5-10 drops sandalwood oil (optional)

1. Mix together the ingredients to make a thick paste. You can adjust the quantities to get the right consistency.
2. Apply to affected area(s) and leave for 15-20 minutes.
3. Wash off whilst gently rubbing in circular motions for exfoliation.
4. Apply a moisturiser.

FREQUENCY

Once a week

Turmeric has been shown to improve areas of hyperpigmentation, possibly due to its compound curcumin inhibiting melanin production. Curcumin is also a potent antioxidant, which can help to protect against free radicals that might cause hyperpigmentation and scars.

Nutmeg contains lignans, specifically macelignan, which has been found to even pigmentation in the skin by inhibiting tyrosinase, which is responsible for melanin production. Ground nutmeg also has a grainy texture that works as a gentle exfoliator, which can help to smooth textured skin caused by scarring.

Sandalwood, like nutmeg, is also potent inhibitor of the enzyme tyrosinase, and can therefore help to reduce hyperpigmentation.

For the benefits of yoghurt or honey, see the previous remedy, and choose whichever best suits your needs.

Liquorice Toner

2 liquorice root sticks OR 1 tsp liquorice root powder
1 cup water

If using liquorice sticks:

1. Bring the water to a boil in a pan and add the liquorice sticks.
2. Simmer on low heat for 5 minutes, then remove from heat.
3. Strain the liquid into a spray bottle or container and refrigerate.
4. Apply to clean skin using the spray bottle or a cotton pad.
5. Follow with moisturiser or your usual skincare routine.

If using liquorice powder:

1. Mix together the water and liquorice powder. Add more water if needed to get a runny consistency.
2. Strain the liquid into a spray bottle or container and refrigerate.
3. Apply to clean skin using the spray bottle or a cotton pad.
4. Follow with moisturiser or your usual skincare routine.

NOTE

Store in the fridge for up to 4 days.

You can also make a mask by mixing the liquorice-infused water with dry ingredients in this section, or by mixing liquorice powder with a runny base like yoghurt or honey. You can even combine liquorice with ingredients that address other skin concerns.

Liquorice has been shown to lighten hyperpigmentation, especially that caused by melasma, inflammatory wounds such as pimples, and UV or sun exposure. This is mainly due to liquiritin and glabridin – two active compounds in liquorice. Liquiritin helps to disperse and remove melanin in the skin, whilst glabridin helps to prevent UV-induced hyperpigmentation, as well as inhibiting tyrosinase activity, which is responsible for melanin formation.

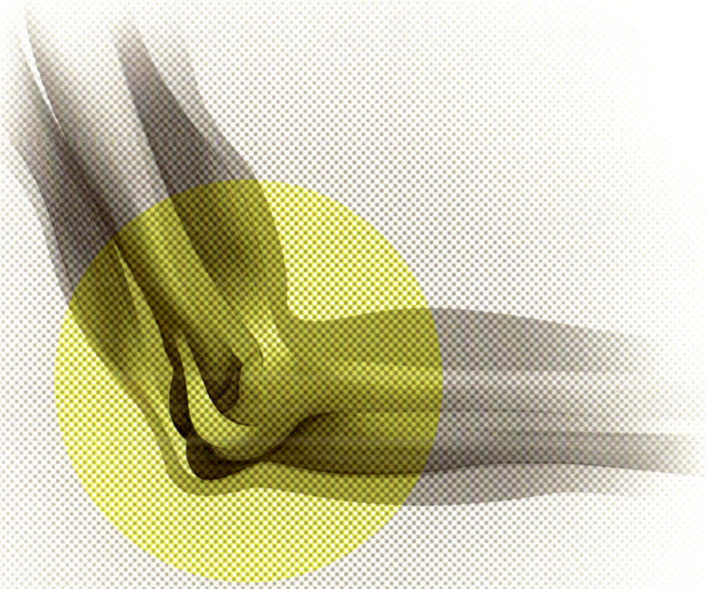

Musculoskeletal

Musculoskeletal Remedies

PAGE 112 Joint Pain & Arthritis

PAGE 124 Muscle Soreness & Cramps

Joint Pain & Arthritis

Note that the remedies in this chapter are interchangeable i.e. muscle soreness remedies may be helpful for joint pain and vice versa. This is because most of the musculoskeletal remedies address pain and inflammation, which is relevant for both joint and muscle problems.

Spice Blend

5 garlic cloves
1 tbsp ground turmeric
½ tsp black pepper
1 tbsp ground ginger
1 tbsp ground OR whole fenugreek seeds
1 tbsp ground celery seeds
1 tbsp ground cinnamon

1. Microwave or roast the garlic for 10-15 seconds with the skin on, then let cool and remove the skin.
2. If using whole fenugreek seeds, dry roast them on low heat for a few minutes. If using ground fenugreek seeds, you can skip this step.
3. Add the garlic, fenugreek, and all the remaining ingredients to a blender.
4. Blend until the garlic is very fine and mixed well with the other ingredients.
5. Store in an airtight container in the fridge.
6. Take 1 heaped teaspoon of this blend every day. You could eat it by itself, add it to hot water, some honey or even a smoothie.

FREQUENCY

1-2 times daily

NOTE

This blend will last 1-2 weeks in the fridge.

Garlic contains a variety of sulphur compounds, which are anti-inflammatory and limit the effects of pro-inflammatory cytokines. This is likely why garlic has been found to improve symptoms of arthritis, such as joint pain and swelling.

Turmeric contains curcumin, a potent antioxidant, anti-inflammatory and immunomodulatory compound shown to be effective at reducing joint and muscle pain as well as improving joint function, including in those with arthritis. Research also shows curcumin to act like TNF and COX-2 inhibitors, which are both commonly used to treat arthritis, including osteoarthritis and rheumatoid arthritis.

Black pepper increases the bioavailability of curcumin in turmeric by up to 2000% i.e. improves the absorption of curcumin. Black pepper also has anti-inflammatory, antioxidant and antiarthritic effects due to its component piperine.

Ginger contains compounds like gingerols and shogaols, which have anti-inflammatory and antioxidant properties, which could explain why ginger has been found to relieve joint and muscle pain and inflammation in those with osteoarthritis and rheumatoid arthritis. Ginger has also been found to function as a COX-2 inhibitor, which is how common arthritis medications work to relieve pain.

Fenugreek seeds have anti-inflammatory and anti-arthritic properties, and have been found to reduce joint swelling, pain and inflammation. Fenugreek also has an oestrogenic effect by binding to oestrogen receptors and functioning like the hormone. This could be helpful as research has linked oestrogen deficiency with arthritis in women, hence why hormone replacement therapy is often used as treatment.

Celery seeds have anti-inflammatory and analgesic effects, and have been found to be as effective as anti-inflammatory drugs in relieving arthritis symptoms like pain and swelling. Celery seed has also been shown to have anti-gout effects, as it contains a substance called luteolin, which blocks an enzyme that contributes to the overproduction of uric acid.

Cinnamon contains cinnamaldehyde – a potent ant-inflammatory – and has been found to improve symptoms of rheumatoid arthritis. This could also be because cinnamon helps to protect regulatory T cells which regulate immune responses and protect against autoimmune diseases. Cinnamon has also been shown to reduce the activity of osteoclasts (cells that cause bone damage) and therefore slow the process of bone loss.

Ginger & Capsaicin Rub

¾ cup coconut oil, melted
1 tsp ginger root powder
1-2 tsp cayenne pepper powder
10 drops lemongrass oil (optional)

1. Mix all the ingredients together thoroughly so that the spices don't clump or settle at the bottom. You can do this by hand or by using a blender.
2. Spoon or pour into a glass jar or container and leave to cool until it starts to solidify. You can also put it in the fridge to make it solidify faster.
3. Rub this ointment on sore or painful areas as needed.

FREQUENCY

Up to 3 times a day

NOTE

You can always replace the cayenne pepper with extra ginger root powder, or reduce the quantities of cayenne and/or ginger to make a less concentrated ointment.

If you want to minimise the greasiness, you can reduce the coconut oil quantity to ¼ cup and add ½ cup shea or cocoa butter. Or you can add 1 tsp arrowroot powder to the mixture in step 1.

Ginger has strong anti-inflammatory properties due to compounds like gingerols and shogaols, and has been shown to improve joint pain and function in those with osteoarthritis. When absorbed by the skin, ginger acts as a COX-2 inhibitor, which is how many arthritis medications work to relieve pain.

Cayenne pepper contains capsaicin, which has been found to ease joint pain when applied every day. This is because capsaicin activates nerve fibres, and with repeated applications, these nerve fibres become desensitised resulting in fewer pain signals being transmitted to the brain.

Lemongrass oil has been found to ease arthritis pain when applied topically, possibly due to the citral it contains, which has anti-inflammatory and analgesic properties.

Omega-3 Seed Mix

½ cup chia seeds
½ cup ground/milled flaxseeds
½ cup hemp seeds

1. Mix together the seeds.
2. Store the mix in an airtight container in a cool, dry place.
3. Consume 1-2 tbsp of this mixture per day. You could add it to smoothies, cereal, yoghurt, salads, soups, or even vegetables.

FREQUENCY

Daily

You can get a ready-made mix of hemp, chia and flax seed from most supermarkets, so you can use this instead of mixing the seeds yourself.

Chia, flax and hemp seeds are all high in anti-inflammatory omega-3 fatty acids, which have been found to relieve joint pain and stiffness when taken regularly, including in those with arthritis. The seeds are also high in fibre, which can help promote a feeling of fullness and therefore help to control weight. This is important as excess weight puts added stress on joints (especially knees) and weight loss in overweight people has been shown to relieve joint pain and slow cartilage degeneration.

Flax Seed Compress

1 tbsp ground/milled flaxseeds
(or you can grind whole flaxseeds yourself)
3 tbsp boiled water
1 tsp ground turmeric (optional)
1 piece of cloth/gauze

1. Mix together all the ingredients. You can make a larger quantity if needed.
2. Stir the mixture until it becomes a thick but spreadable consistency.
3. Spread the mixture on the affected area and press the cloth on top.
4. Hold it there or secure with tape or string for 2-4 hours.
5. Remove the compress and wash or wipe off the paste.

FREQUENCY

As often as needed

For extra protection, you can add another piece of cloth or plastic on top of the first piece of cloth and secure it with the tape or string.

Flaxseed has been found to reduce pain and increase joint function when applied topically for those with osteoarthritis, and was found more effective at reducing carpal tunnel syndrome symptoms – a type of repetitive strain injury – than a splint. This is likely due to flaxseed's high omega-3 fatty acid content, specifically alpha-linolenic acid (ALA), which has anti-inflammatory and analgesic effects.

Pranayama (Anulom Vilom)

1 Take a deep breath in through your left nostril whilst closing your right nostril with your thumb.

2 Hold for a few seconds, then breathe out through your right nostril whilst closing your left nostril with two fingers.

3 Then, breathe in through your right nostril, hold, and exhale through your left nostril.

FREQUENCY

Repeat this process for 10 minutes at least once a day

Deep breathing has been found to alleviate both short-term and chronic pain by relaxing the body. It helps to relax the muscles that often tense up as a result of pain, which in turn further aggravates the pain. Deep breathing also lowers the body's stress response; this is important as stress sets off the body's inflammatory response and can therefore fuel joint damage, especially in those with joint pain associated with autoimmune or inflammatory diseases like rheumatoid arthritis.

Yoga (Sukshma Vyayama)

This form of yoga essentially consists of light movements ('sukshma vyayama' literally means 'subtle yoga'), much like stretching, and puts less stress on the joints than other forms of yoga. The following are some examples of movements you can do. Any of these movements should be repeated 5-10 times daily, but do them during your least painful time of the day.

Ankles

Ankle Flexion: Flex and point the foot gently, then relax.
Ankle Circles: trace a circle with your toes clockwise, then anti-clockwise.

Knees

NOTE

You can hold on to a chair or wall to support your balance. You can also do these lying down (on your back for knee hug, on your front for quad stretch).

Knee Hug: Whilst standing, hug one knee to your chest and hold for 10 seconds. Then do this with the other leg.

Standing Quad Stretch: Reverse the above exercise by bringing the heel of one leg up to your bottom with your hand and holding for 10 seconds. Then do this with the other leg.

Hips

Butterfly Stretch: Sit on the floor with the soles of your feet together and try to gently push your knees out to the side whilst keeping your feet together until you get resistance (but not pain). Hold this for 10 seconds then relax.

Bridging: Lie on your back with your knees bent and feet flat on the floor. Lift your pelvis and lower back off the floor. Hold this for 5 seconds then lower down slowly.

Wrists

Wrist Rolls: Make a fist on each hand and rotate your wrists clockwise and anti-clockwise.

Wrist Stretch: Hold your right arm out with your palm facing down and towards your body, so your fingers are pointing towards the floor. Using your left hand, gently push the right hand towards you until you feel a stretch. Hold for a few seconds then repeat this on the other side.

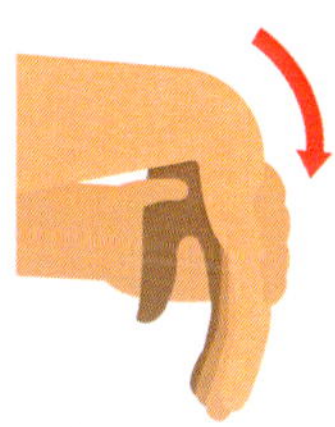

Fingers

Fist Clench: Make a fist and very gently squeeze, then release. Do this on both sides.

Finger Lifts: Place your hand flat on the table, palm facing down. Lift each finger off the table one-by-one, hold for a couple of seconds, then lower it. Do this on both sides.

Elbows

Bicep Curls: Stand up and have your arms by your side, then bend your arms slowly upwards so that your hands are touching your shoulder, but keeping your upper arms by your side. Hold for 15-20 seconds then relax. You can add a weight if it's too easy.

Arm Extensions: Breathe in whilst extending your arms in front of you, as if pushing away from your body, keeping them parallel to the floor. Breathe out whilst bringing your arms back towards your body, turning your palms to face towards you.

Shoulders

Shoulder Rotations: Roll your shoulders forwards and then backwards. You can do this with your arms bent and your fingers on your shoulders, or with straight arms.

Overhead Tricep Extensions: Lift your arms above your head and bring your hands together. Then bend your arms at the elbow, reaching your hands over the head and down the back. Hold for a few seconds, then relax. You can also do this one arm at a time, and add a weight if you like. Make sure not to arch your back.

Neck

Side to Side: Slowly look to your right, then to your left.

Neck Tilt: Hold Slowly tilt your head towards one shoulder, whilst looking straight ahead and keeping your shoulder down. Hold for a few seconds, then tilt your head to the other side.

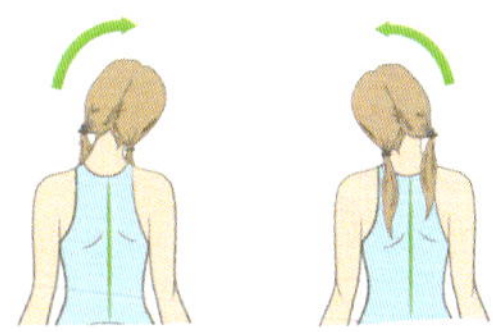

Neck Drop & Raise: Slowly drop your head forward so your chin touches your chest, hold for a few seconds, then lean your head back and hold for a few seconds.

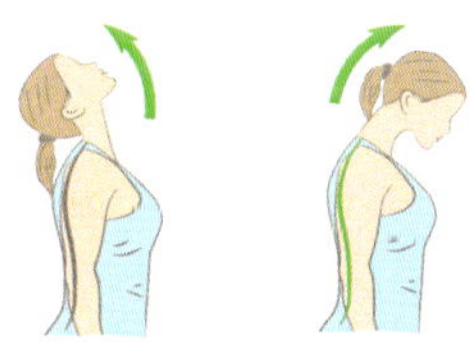

Neck Retraction: Sit or stand up straight. Looking straight ahead, pull your chin straight in, as if to make a double chin. You should feel this stretch in the back of your neck and possibly down your upper back. Hold for a few seconds, then relax.

Yoga has been shown to improve quality of life and increase energy in those with chronic joint pain, including arthritis. This particular form of yoga can help to relieve joint and muscle pain as it essentially involves stretching. Stretching is known to loosen stiff joints and improve the range of motion, and, when done regularly, can help to strengthen the muscles that support the joints.

Muscle Soreness & Cramps

Blueberry Smoothie

1 cup blueberries
Base liquid e.g. almond milk, soya milk, dairy milk, yoghurt
Any additional extras e.g. bananas, nuts, seeds, cinnamon, ice

1. Blend all the ingredients until smooth. Add more solids or liquids to get your desired consistency.
2. Drink before or after exercise.

FREQUENCY

Up to 3 times a day

NOTE

If you don't like smoothies, you can eat 1 cup of blueberries by themselves, with yoghurt, or however you prefer.

Blueberries contain powerful antioxidant and anti-inflammatory properties, and can therefore help the muscles relax and recover by reducing the localised oxidative stress and inflammation that can often occur after exercise. This is likely why studies have found that having a blueberry smoothie before and/or after exercise helps to accelerate exercise-induced muscle damage recovery.

Turmeric, Cinnamon & Ginger Spice Mix

2 tbsp ground cinnamon
2 tbsp ground ginger
2 tbsp ground turmeric
1 tsp black pepper

1. Mix together all the ingredients. Store them in an airtight container at room temperature.
2. Consume 1-2 teaspoons of this spice mix a day – you can add it to hot water, eat it with honey, add it to smoothies, or include it in your cooking.

FREQUENCY

Daily

NOTE

The spice mix will stay for at least 6 months, so you can make a larger quantity of the mix in the same proportions if you prefer.

> Turmeric, cinnamon and ginger all contain curcumin, which has potent anti-inflammatory and antioxidant properties, whilst cinnamon and ginger have additional compounds with the same effects, like cinnamaldehyde, gingerols and shogaols. Curcumin has been shown to ease muscle pain, swelling and inflammation when taken daily, whilst cinnamon and ginger have been found to reduce exercise-induced muscle soreness.

Black pepper increases the bioavailability of curcumin in turmeric by up to 2000% i.e. improves the absorption of curcumin. Black pepper also has anti-inflammatory, and antioxidant properties, so it can potentially reduce the oxidative stress and inflammation associated with muscle soreness and cramps.

Camphor & Clove Oil Massage

½ tsp white camphor oil OR 2 pieces camphor
15 drops clove oil OR 3-4 cloves
¼ cup coconut oil, melted OR olive oil
1 glass, airtight jar or dropper bottle (use a dark glass jar, but if you only have clear, then put it in a paper bag and store it in a dark place)

If using camphor oil:

1. Mix the camphor oil and clove oil with the melted coconut oil or the olive oil.
2. Pour the oil blend into the glass jar or dropper bottle.
3. Apply to the affected area(s) and massage the area(s) with gradually increasing pressure. Stop or reduce pressure if you find it painful.

If using camphor pieces:

1. Warm the coconut oil in a pan on low heat.
2. Add the camphor pieces to the pan and stir until they dissolve.
3. Remove from heat and mix in the clove oil.
4. Pour the oil blend into the glass jar or dropper bottle.
5. Apply to the affected area(s) and massage the area(s) with gradually increasing pressure. Stop or reduce pressure if you find it painful.

If using cloves:

Replace the clove oil in the instructions with the cloves, and leave the mixture in the bottle for 7-10 days before using. You can then remove the cloves or leave them in the bottle.

FREQUENCY

As often as needed

SHORTCUT

Use Vicks VapoRub instead of the oil blend as it contains camphor oil.

NOTE

This oil blend will keep for about 4 months.

> Camphor is a common ingredient in topical analgesics, as it is antispasmodic and anti-inflammatory, helping to relieve muscle spasms, cramps, stiffness and soreness. Camphor provides both cooling and warming sensations, as the oil cools and numbs nerve endings, which reduces pain, then warms the area by increasing circulation, which helps to relax tight muscles. As well as providing short-term relief, camphor oil has been found effective in reducing chronic muscle and joint pain.

> Clove oil is often used to treat muscle pain due to its analgesic compound called eugenol. The oil also has a warming effect on muscles by increasing circulation, which helps to reduce muscle tension and improve movement.

Massage helps to relax muscle cramping, soreness and pain by increasing blood flow to the affected region, helping to reduce inflammation and any swelling in the area. Massage has been found to be effective in chronic conditions, like arthritis, and exercise-induced or short-term muscle damage.

Papaya & Pineapple

¼-½ papaya
1 cup pineapple

Eat the papaya and pineapple every day. You can have it by itself, in a smoothie, or make a fruit salad or dessert.

FREQUENCY

Once daily

Papaya is rich in antioxidants like vitamin C, and papain, an anti-inflammatory compound, which help to reduce inflammation and oxidative stress in muscles and joints, therefore alleviating soreness, pain and stiffness. It's specifically been found effective when combined with enzymes including bromelain (which is found in pineapple). Papain has also been found to be immunomodulatory, increasing regulatory T-cells in those with rheumatoid arthritis.

Pineapple contains bromelain, a compound found to have anti-inflammatory, analgesic and immunomodulatory properties, hence why it has been found effective for relieving pain, soft-tissue swelling and joint stiffness. Like papaya, pineapple is also rich in vitamin C, an antioxidant which has been shown to reduce muscle soreness and pain, including that associated with rheumatoid arthritis.

Coconut Water

2 cups unsweetened or pure coconut water
¼ tsp sea salt (optional)
1 squeeze lemon or lime juice (optional)

1. Mix together all the ingredients.
2. Drink during and/or after exercise, or at the first sign of cramping.

FREQUENCY

No more than 1 litre a day

If you don't like the taste of coconut water, you can add the optional ingredients above, or mix coconut water with another fruit juice.

Coconut water is rich in electrolytes like potassium and magnesium, and has been shown to rehydrate and replenish electrolytes after exercise more effectively than water and as effectively as high-electrolyte sports drinks. This is important as electrolytes help the muscles to work more smoothly, and electrolyte imbalances or deficiencies have been associated with muscle cramps. Coconut water can therefore help reduce susceptibility to muscle cramping.

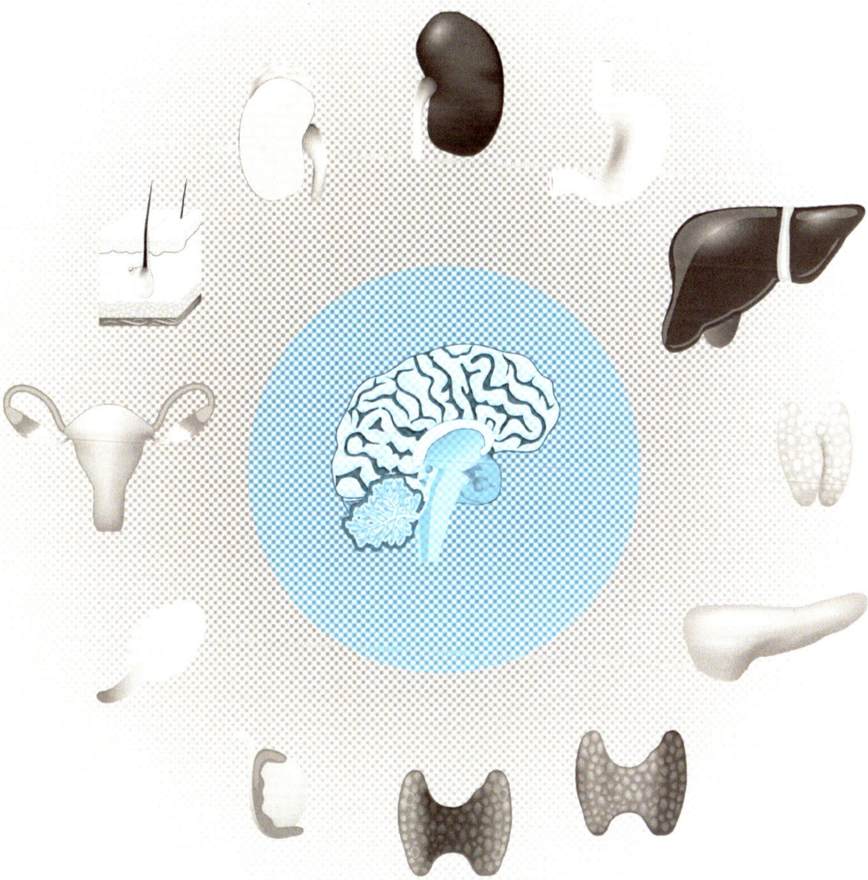

Metabolic & Endocrine

Metabolic & Endocrine Remedies

PAGE 132 Overweight

PAGE 136 Underweight

PAGE 140 High Blood Sugar

PAGE 143 High Cholesterol

PAGE 146 Thyroid Disease

Overweight

In addition to some remedies, this section outlines lifestyle and diet changes. Whilst different things will work for different people, the following recommendations involve simple, effective changes that are fairly easy to stick to over time. Consistency is key!

Adjust Your Diet

Reduce your intake of refined carbohydrates. The main sources of refined carbs are cereals, pastries, sweets, sugary snacks, white bread, and added sugar. You can replace these with whole grains. Consume more fruits and vegetables.

> Refined carbs are low in fibre and digested quickly, causing rapid spikes in blood sugar and insulin levels, which only provides short-term fullness followed by a blood sugar drop and hunger soon after eating. Long-term studies have also linked refined carbs to increased belly fat.

> Fruits and vegetables are high in water, nutrients and fibre, and usually have a very low energy density. This makes it possible to eat large servings without consuming many calories.

Drink More Water

Aim to drink 1.5-2 litres of water per day and try to drink more water before meals. Replace any sugary drinks with water.

If you still want a sweetened drink, you can add some lemon and honey to the water.

Several studies have found that drinking water can increase the amount of calories burned by 24-30% for an hour afterwards. It can also reduce appetite before eating a meal, therefore decreasing calorie intake, helping with weight loss. As water is calorie-free, replacing high-calorie, sugary drinks with water is an effective way to cut calorie intake.

Daily Exercise

Aim to do 20-30 minutes of cardio every day – this can be anything from a brisk walk to jogging to swimming to dancing. Try to choose an activity you enjoy as you'll be more likely to stick to it. To avoid losing too much muscle mass you can also incorporate resistance training a few times a week, whether it's weights or pushups and situps.

Exercising not only helps burn off extra calories and body fat, but also minimises the muscle loss that can result from dieting. This is important as muscle is more metabolically active than fat, meaning that it can boost the metabolism and help lose and keep weight off better.

Smaller Plates

Use smaller plates when serving food to encourage yourself to eat smaller portions without feeling deprived.

Studies have shown that using smaller plates helps people eat less because it changes how they see portion sizes. People also tend to fill their plates regardless of size, so taking a smaller plate helps reduce food consumption whilst feeling like it's a normal sized portion.

Fenugreek Tea

1 tbsp fenugreek seeds
1-2 cups water

1 Boil the water in a pan.
2 Lower the flame, add the fenugreek seeds, and simmer for about 5 minutes.
3 Strain the tea into a mug and drink every morning.

If you don't like hot drinks, you can soak the fenugreek seeds in cold water (same quantities) and leave overnight. Then filter out the seeds in the morning and drink.

Studies have shown that fenugreek can support weight loss by reducing fat intake and appetite. This could be due to galactomannan, a water-soluble component in the seeds found to suppress appetite.

Black Pepper

There are a number of ways you can consume black pepper:

- Add ½ tsp ground black pepper to water or herbal tea.
- Chew 2-3 black peppercorns (if you can handle the strong taste). Make sure to drink a cup of water afterwards for this method.
- Add ½-1 tsp ground black pepper to vegetable or fruit juices.
- Eat ½ tsp ground black pepper mixed with 1 tsp honey.

FREQUENCY

Every day on an empty stomach, no more than 3 times a day

Black pepper contains piperine, which has been found to raise the metabolic rate through thermogenesis. This means the body converts more nutrients into energy rather than stored fat. Piperine has also been found to increase lipolysis (the process by which fats are broken down) and inhibit the formation of fat cells, leading to a decrease in fat mass and unhealthy levels of fat in the blood.

Underweight

Frequent Snacks

Have small snacks more often but keep them healthy such as nuts, cheese, yoghurt or avocado. See the end of this section (page 138-139) for a couple of snack ideas.

> To put on weight, you need to eat more calories than your body burns, so additional snacks are an easy way to increase your calorie intake, even if you don't have a large appetite. Nuts are calorie-dense and rich in healthy fats. Cheese is high in calories, healthy fats and protein, as is yoghurt and avocado.

More Milk

Drink more full-fat milk – the best times to have it are after exercise and just before bed. You can drink it by itself or add it to things like smoothies, cereals or soups. Banana smoothies are a good and healthy option as bananas can add calories whilst supplying important nutrients.

> Milk is a rich source of calories and high-quality proteins such as whey and casein. Studies have shown that drinking it after exercise can help build muscle mass and support healthy weight gain. Furthermore, growth hormone – which boosts muscle growth is elevated during sleep, so drinking milk before bed helps to maximise growth as the milk protein provides the amino acids required for muscle growth.

Resistance Training

Aim to do resistance training 2-4 times a week, whether it's with weights or bodyweight exercises like pushups and situps. Don't cut out your cardio – do 30 minutes of cardio 3 times a week or a shorter, brisk walk every day, but avoid doing cardio before resistance training.

> Resistance training will make sure that excess calories go to your muscle cells instead of only fat cells. Doing some cardio is also important to keep up general fitness and wellbeing, provided it's not so excessive that it burns all the extra calories being eaten.

Bigger Plates

Use bigger plates when serving food to encourage yourself to eat larger portions.

> Studies have shown that people tend to fill their plates regardless of size, so taking a larger plate encourages an increase in serving size whilst feeling like it's a normal-sized portion.

More Protein

Add in high-protein foods to your diet such as lentils, cottage cheese (paneer), fish, eggs, soy, dairy products, or nuts. But don't go overboard and add in too much as proteins are very filling, so it can reduce your hunger and appetite, making it harder to consume enough calories.

> Protein forms the building blocks of muscles so eating sufficient protein is essential to gain muscle weight rather than just fat.

Below are a couple of typical Indian high-protein snacks:

Lassi

1-2 cups full-fat OR Greek yoghurt (has almost twice the protein of regular yoghurt)
½ cup milk (cow's milk, soy, or almond milk) OR water

The remaining ingredients depend on the flavour you want:

- Sweet: Add 2 tsp sugar, honey or sweetener of your choice
- Savoury: Add ½ tsp salt and ½ tsp ground cumin
- Mango: Add 1 chopped mango and ¼ tsp ground cardamom (optional)
- Banana: Add 1 banana and ¼ tsp ground cardamom (optional)

1 Mix all the ingredients in a blender until smooth.
2 Taste and add seasoning as needed e.g. more salt or sugar.
3 Pour into a glass and drink.

Crunchy Roasted Chickpeas

1 can chickpeas, drained and rinsed
Olive oil
Salt
Spices of your choice e.g. cumin, black pepper, paprika, garam masala, cinnamon (get creative – you can even make them sweet by adding sugar)

1. Preheat oven to 200°C.
2. Pat dry the chickpeas with kitchen towel or a tea towel. The drier they are, the crispier they will get.
3. Spread the chickpeas on a baking tray and toss with some olive oil and salt.
4. Roast in the oven for about 30 minutes, or until golden and crisp, making sure to toss them halfway through.

   NOTE

   Ovens can vary so cook for longer if the chickpeas aren't crispy enough.

5. Remove from oven and whilst warm, toss with any spices you are using.
6. Let the chickpeas cool, then store in an airtight container. They are best eaten within a week.

You can use this same recipe to make spiced nuts, but they only need 10-15 minutes in the oven until golden.

High Blood Sugar

Fenugreek Water

1 tsp fenugreek seeds
1 cup water

Method 1:

1. Soak the seeds in the water.
2. Leave overnight.
3. Strain out the seeds and drink the water in the morning, ideally on an empty stomach. You can also eat the seeds if you want.

Method 2:

1. Dry roast a larger amount (at least 1 cup) of fenugreek seeds for 2-3 minutes in a pan.
2. Grind to a powder and store in an airtight container.
3. Add 1 teaspoon of the powder to warm water and drink every morning.

FREQUENCY

Once daily

You can also make fenugreek tea by brewing the seeds in boiling water for 5 minutes, then straining.

Fenugreek seeds are high in fibre, which helps to slow digestion and the body's absorption of carbohydrates and sugar. Research has found fenugreek seeds to reduce fasting blood sugar levels, improve glucose tolerance and reduce insulin resistance, and be effective for those with type 1 and 2 diabetes as well as prediabetes.

Turmeric, Cinnamon & Ginger Spice Mix

2 tbsp ground cinnamon
2 tbsp ground ginger
2 tbsp ground turmeric
1 tsp ground black pepper

1. Mix together all the ingredients.
2. Store them in an airtight container at room temperature.
3. Consume 1-2 teaspoons of this spice mix a day – you can add it to hot water, eat it with honey, add it to smoothies, or include it in your cooking.

FREQUENCY

Daily

NOTE

The spice mix will stay for at least 6 months, so you can make a larger quantity of the mix in the same proportions if you prefer.

Turmeric's active component, curcumin, has been found to reduce blood sugar levels by a number of mechanisms, like increasing glucose uptake from the blood and reducing glucose production. Curcumin has also been found to reduce insulin resistance and protect insulin-producing cells from dysfunction.

Ginger has been found to improve the uptake of glucose into muscle cells without using insulin, as well as reducing insulin resistance in those with type 2 diabetes, therefore helping to reduce high blood sugar.

Cinnamon helps to lower blood sugar by imitating insulin and increasing glucose transport to cells. In addition to reducing fasting blood sugar, cinnamon has been found to minimise the blood sugar spikes that often occur after eating, possibly by slowing stomach emptying and blocking enzymes that break down carbohydrates in the small intestine.

Black pepper increases the bioavailability of curcumin in turmeric by up to 2000% i.e. improves the absorption of curcumin, as it is otherwise poorly absorbed by the body.

High Cholesterol

Aside from dietary recommendations you likely would have received from your doctor, such as cutting fats or using unrefined oil in cooking, below are some additional remedies for reducing high cholesterol. If you are even slightly overweight, losing some weight can help to lower cholesterol – see pages 132-135 for relevant remedies.

Cinnamon & Flaxseed Powder

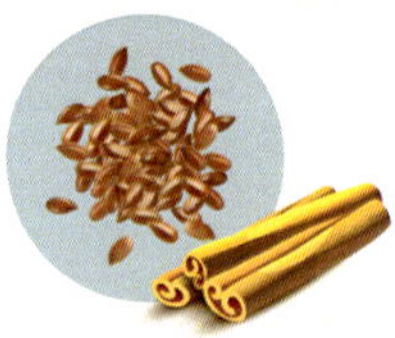

3 tbsp flaxseed powder
1 tbsp ground cinnamon

1 Combine the flaxseed powder and ground cinnamon.

2 Consume 1-2 tbsp of this mixture daily. It can be put in cereal, smoothies, baked into bread and so on.

> Research has shown that consuming flaxseed powder daily for 3 months can lower 'bad' LDL cholesterol by almost 20%, whilst increasing 'good' HDL cholesterol. The fibre in flax seeds binds to bile salts which are excreted by the body, and cholesterol is pulled from the blood into the liver to replenish these salts, which lowers the blood levels of cholesterol. The omega-3 fatty acid, ALA, in flaxseeds can also prevent cholesterol from being deposited in the blood vessels of the heart and reduce inflammation in the arteries.

> Cinnamon reduces LDL cholesterol and triglycerides, whilst keeping HDL levels stable, though the mechanism for how this works is not yet clear.

Dark Chocolate

90% cocoa dark chocolate

Consume 20-25g of dark chocolate daily. You can eat it by itself, in cereal, in a smoothie, with fruits, or get creative.

> Cocoa powder has been found to significantly reduce 'bad' LDL cholesterol and increase 'good' HDL cholesterol. It also reduces oxidative damage to LDL due to the abundance of antioxidants in dark chocolate. This is important as oxidised LDL is capable of damaging other tissues, like the lining of the heart.

Pranayama (Kapalbhati)

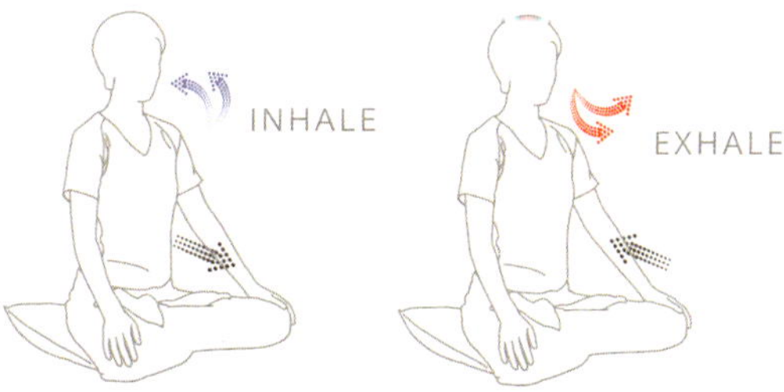

1. Sit upright, close your eyes and take a deep breath in.
2. Expel the breath with many rapid, forceful contractions of the abdominal muscles until all breath has been exhaled.
3. Then take a deep breath and exhale slowly.
4. Repeat this process for 10 minutes.

FREQUENCY

Daily

NOTE

Do not do this within an hour after eating.

> Yoga and pranayama have been found to reduce 'bad' LDL cholesterol and also improve 'good' HDL cholesterol levels in diabetics. Research has also found that those who regularly practiced yoga and pranayama showed significant improvement in LDL, HDL cholesterol and blood pressure.

Thyroid Disease

As hypothyroidism and hyperthyroidism have a variety of complex causes, other sections of this book, such as immune system problems, insomnia, fatigue, and so on, may also be helpful for managing symptoms or addressing causes.

Pranayama (Singhasan)

1. Kneel on the floor on all fours and inhale slowly through the nose.
2. Exhale forcefully, whilst sticking your tongue out towards your chin and making a long 'ha' sound or a roaring sound.
3. Breathe normally for a few moments.
4. Repeat this 5-10 times and finish by deep breathing for a couple minutes.

FREQUENCY

1-2 times daily

You can also do this in a seated position on a chair or cross-legged with your hands placed on your knees.

> Research has shown yoga and pranayama to have a positive effect on improving thyroid function and managing the related symptoms. It can also help to relieve stress – a factor linked to hypothyroidism.

Pressure Point

1. Press firmly with your thumb on the pressure points shown below.
2. Hold for five seconds then release.
3. Repeat three times for each hand. Do this for one hand at a time.

> The goal of acupressure is to restore health and balance to other body parts via different pressure points. Whilst most of the supporting evidence is anecdotal, it's a non-invasive, nonpharmaceutical therapy with no side effects so is worth trying.

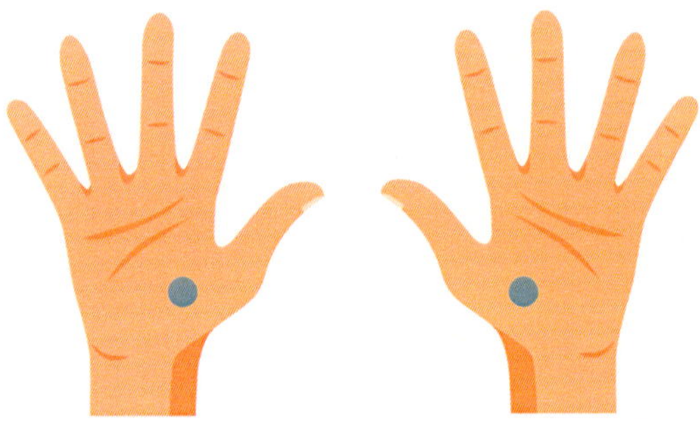

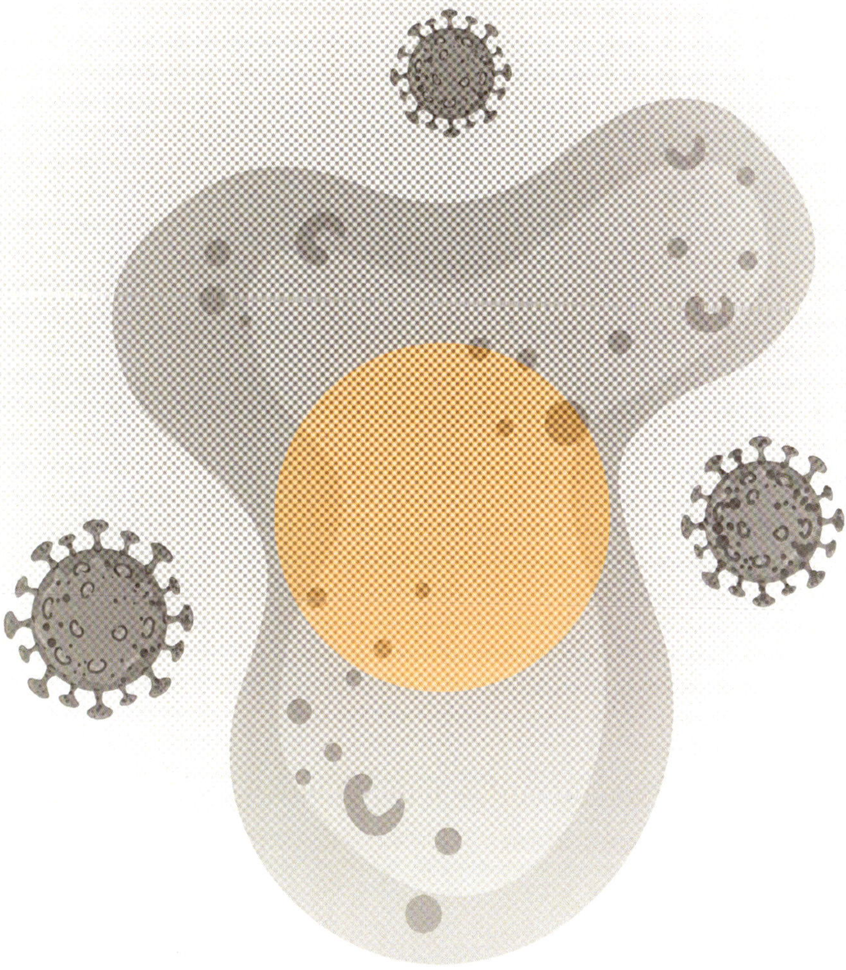

Immune System

Immune System Remedies

PAGE 150 Weak Immune System

PAGE 158 Hay Fever

Weak Immune System

Spiced Herbal Tea

Quantities below are for 2 servings

1 tsp black pepper
1 tsp cumin seeds
1 clove
1 cinnamon stick OR ½ tsp ground cinnamon
1 tsp ground turmeric
1 tsp raw honey
1 tsp fresh ginger, chopped
8 mint leaves
4 raisins (optional)
4 cups water

1. Dry roast the black pepper, cumin seeds, clove, and cinnamon stick on a low flame for about 30 seconds in a pan.
2. Add the water, turmeric, honey, ginger, mint leaves and raisins (if using).
3. Boil for about 10 minutes or until the water reduces to roughly half the quantity.
4. Strain and drink one cup of this daily.

FREQUENCY

Once daily

If there is any extra liquid, strain it into a glass container or jar and store in the fridge for up to 2 days. Warm it thoroughly before drinking – either in the microwave or a pan.

Black pepper is rich in antioxidants such as piperine, which help prevent free radical damage to healthy cells. It is also antibacterial, and can help relieve coughs and colds by acting as an expectorant (clears mucus). Black pepper also helps the body absorb essential nutrients, as well as the curcumin in turmeric.

Cumin seeds have anti-inflammatory and antiseptic properties. They also contain substances – apigenin and luteolin – which act as antioxidants i.e. they defend against the free radicals that attack healthy cells.

Cloves have antimicrobial, anti-inflammatory and anti-viral properties. Cloves also contain eugenol – a natural antioxidant found to be more effective than vitamin E – which helps the immune system fight oxidative damage caused by free radicals.

Cinnamon has antifungal and antibacterial properties due to the presence of cinnamaldehyde, and also contains antioxidants. Cinnamon also protects regulatory T cells which regulate immune responses and help prevent autoimmune diseases.

Turmeric contains curcumin, which has anti-inflammatory, antibacterial and antioxidant properties, and has been shown to help treat and prevent several chronic conditions. Turmeric can also help with immunomodulation i.e. keeping different immune cells in balance to enable the immune system to function correctly.

Honey contains phytonutrients with antioxidant, antimicrobial and antifungal properties. Notably, research has found honey to be more effective than various over-the-counter medicines and antibiotics for respiratory tract infections. Honey also helps reduce cell proliferation which is key to stopping viruses.

Ginger is packed with anti-inflammatory, antioxidant compounds, such as gingerols and shogaols, and also has powerful antiviral and antibacterial properties. This is likely why ginger has been found to enhance immune response and fight chronic inflammation.

Mint has antioxidant and anti-inflammatory properties because of its phytonutrients such as rosmarinic acid. Mint also contains antibacterial compounds which can help fight any harmful bacteria within the GI tract.

Raisins are a rich source of polyphenols, which act as antioxidants. Raisins are also a good source of vitamins and minerals which help boost the immune system, such as iron, calcium and copper.

Ginger Garlic Shot

1-2 garlic cloves
1 inch fresh ginger
1-2 carrots
½ lemon (optional)

1 Juice all the ingredients.

2 Pour into a shot glass and drink (if you're not using a shot glass, it's about 3 tbsp).

3 Store any remaining juice in the fridge for up to 3 days.

FREQUENCY

Up to 3 times daily

If you don't own a juicer, you can use a blender instead then strain with a sieve.

Garlic contains a number of compounds which have been found to strengthen the immune system and boost the disease-fighting response of white blood cells when they encounter viruses, such as those that cause colds or the flu. Garlic also has an immunomodulatory effect by regulating inflammation, and so can help treat or prevent autoimmune diseases.

Ginger is packed with anti-inflammatory, antioxidant compounds, such as gingerols and shogaols, and also has powerful antiviral and antibacterial properties. This is why ginger has been found to enhance immune response and fight chronic inflammation.

Carrots are rich in vitamins A and C – antioxidants which help to protect immune cells from free radical damage. Carrots are also high in vitamin B6, which is essential for immune cell proliferation and antibody production.

Garlic Milk

2 garlic cloves, chopped
1 cup milk (for dairy-free, use coconut, almond or soy milk)
1 tbsp honey

1. Bring the milk to a boil in a pan.
2. Add the garlic and honey and mix well.
3. Remove from heat and leave for 10 minutes.
4. Strain the milk and drink warm.

FREQUENCY

Once daily

NOTE

This isn't the tastiest drink, so you may want to reserve drinking it for when you feel like you're about to come down with something (or if you're already ill).

You can add extras like turmeric and black pepper or ginger for added benefits.

Garlic contains a number of compounds which have been found to strengthen the immune system and boost the disease-fighting response of white blood cells when they encounter viruses, such as those that cause colds or the flu. Garlic also has an immunomodulatory effect by regulating inflammation, and so can help treat or prevent autoimmune diseases.

Honey contains phytonutrients which are responsible for its antioxidant, antimicrobial and antifungal properties and can help boost the immune system. Notably, research has found honey to be more effective than various over-the-counter medicines and antibiotics for respiratory tract infections. Honey also helps reduce cell proliferation which is key to stopping viruses.

Golden Milk

1-2 tsp ground turmeric
¼ tsp ground black pepper
½ inch fresh ginger, grated
½-1 tsp honey (adjust to taste)
2-4 cardamom pods, crushed
OR ½ tsp ground cardamom (optional)
2 cups milk (for dairy-free, use coconut, almond or soy milk)

1 Add the milk to a pan over medium heat.

2 When the milk is warm, add the turmeric, ground black pepper, ginger, honey, and cardamom.

3 Simmer on low heat for 5 minutes.

4 Strain into a mug and drink.

Note: You may get a film or 'skin' over the top as it cools in the mug, but you can just remove this with a spoon or push it to the side.

FREQUENCY

Once or twice daily

NOTE

You can add the turmeric, black pepper and honey to the milk and heat it all up in the microwave, though you'll miss out on the benefits of the ginger.

You can even use water instead of milk (though it won't be as tasty).

Turmeric contains curcumin, which has anti-inflammatory, antibacterial and antioxidant properties, and has been shown to help treat and prevent several chronic conditions. Turmeric can also help with immunomodulation i.e. keeping different immune cells in balance to enable the immune system to function correctly.

Black pepper is rich in antioxidants such as piperine, which help prevent free radical damage to healthy cells. It is also antibacterial, and can help relieve coughs and colds by acting as an expectorant (clears mucus). Black pepper also helps the body absorb essential nutrients, as well as the curcumin in turmeric.

Ginger is packed with anti-inflammatory, antioxidant compounds, such as gingerols and shogaols, and also has powerful antiviral and antibacterial properties. This is why ginger has been found to enhance immune response and fight chronic inflammation.

Honey contains phytonutrients which are responsible for its antioxidant, antimicrobial and antifungal power. Notably, research has found honey to be more effective than various over-the-counter medicines and antibiotics for respiratory tract infections. Honey also helps reduce cell proliferation which is key to stopping viruses.

Pranayama (Anulom Vilom)

1. Take a deep breath in through your left nostril whilst closing your right nostril with your thumb.
2. Hold for a few seconds, then breathe out through your right nostril whilst closing your left nostril with two fingers.
3. Then, breathe in through your right nostril, hold, and exhale through your left nostril.

FREQUENCY

Repeat this process for 10 minutes a day

The main proven benefit of this deep breathing technique is relaxing the body and reducing stress. Stress keeps the immune system from functioning at full capacity, and makes the body more susceptible to numerous conditions, including autoimmune diseases.

Get Your Greens

Consume more green vegetables in your diet, especially dark leafy greens (e.g. spinach, kale, arugula) and cruciferous vegetables (e.g. cabbage, cauliflower, broccoli).

Green vegetables are a rich source of fibre, folate, iron, calcium, and vitamins C and K, which all help to boost the immune system. Green vegetables are also the source of a chemical signal that is critical for immune system function as it ensures that certain immune cells in the gut and skin function properly.

Hay Fever

Honey, Turmeric & Black Pepper Booster

½ cup raw honey
2 tbsp ground turmeric
½ tsp black pepper
¼ tsp salt (optional – adjust to taste)

1 Mix all the ingredients together.

2 Consume 1 tablespoon of this mixture daily during allergy season.

NOTE

Store in an airtight container in the fridge for up to 3 weeks.

There are lots of different ways to consume this – by itself, in a smoothie, spread on toast, or mixing it into some hot water or milk.

Turmeric contains curcumin, a phytochemical with powerful antioxidant and anti-inflammatory actions, which can therefore help to relieve swelling and irritation caused by hay fever. It also helps to eradicate allergens from the body, thus aiding faster recovery.

Black pepper increases the bioavailability of curcumin in turmeric by up to 2000% i.e. improves the absorption of curcumin.

Hay fever causes inflammation to the lining of the nose and the protective tissue of the eyes, as well as the throat and sinuses. Honey has been found to reduce symptoms of hay fever, most likely due to its anti-inflammatory properties.

Pollen Blocker Balm

Vaseline
OR
Coconut oil

1. Apply the Vaseline or coconut oil around your nostrils and on the inside edges before going outside.
2. Leave on for the day and wash off when you get back home.

FREQUENCY

Daily during allergy season

Petroleum jelly or coconut oil around the nose acts as a barrier to trap pollen before breathing it in. This works as they are occlusive, meaning they sit on the skin instead of getting absorbed, which creates the barrier.

Turmeric Water

½ tsp ground turmeric
1 cup water

1. Put the turmeric in a glass of water but don't stir it in.
2. Let the turmeric settle at the bottom of the glass (this takes about 20 minutes).
3. Using your finger or a cotton swab, dab some of the turmeric-infused water in the lower waterline of your eyes.

FREQUENCY

Once or twice daily

> Turmeric can help reduce inflammation in the eyes and has been shown to be effective against allergic conjunctivitis – a common issue for those with hay fever. The curcumin in turmeric also has antibacterial properties which help prevent or remedy any further infection in the eye.

Vitamin C

Consume more vitamin C; good sources include oranges, pineapple, papaya, grapefruits, kiwis, sweet yellow peppers and strawberries.

> Vitamin C is considered to be a natural antihistamine because it inhibits the release of histamine by mast cells. Eating foods high in vitamin C has been shown to decrease the irritation of the upper respiratory tract caused by pollen.

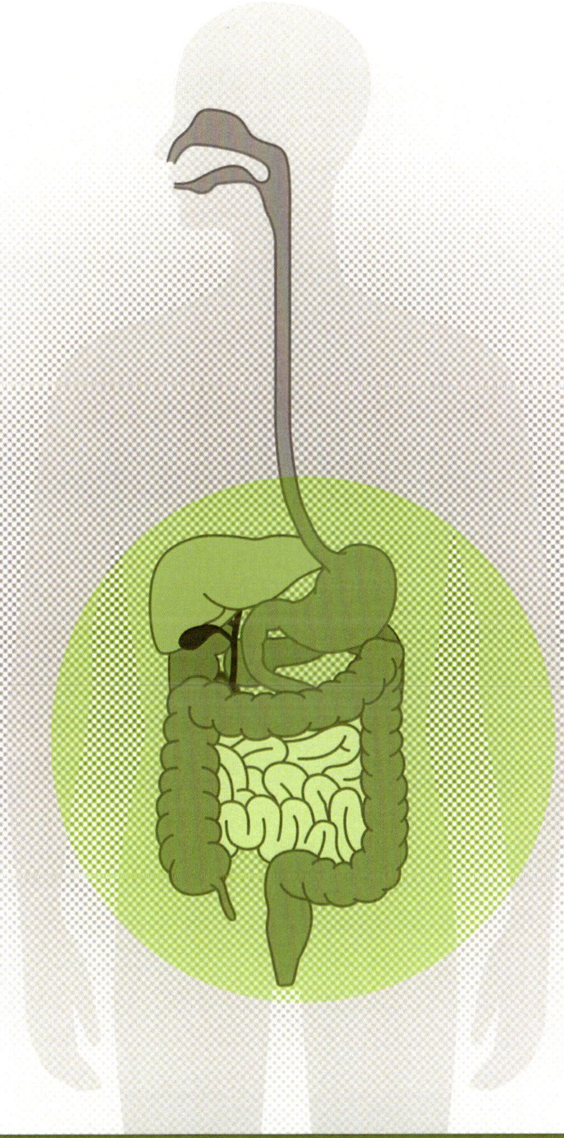

Digestive & Urinary

Digestive & Urinary Remedies

PAGE 164 Constipation

PAGE 168 Diarrhoea

PAGE 174 Gassiness & Bloating

PAGE 178 Heartburn

PAGE 185 Stomach Ache Or Pain

PAGE 189 Urinary Tract Infections (UTIs)

PAGE 191 Urinary Incontinence

PAGE 194 Vomiting & Nausea

Constipation

Dietary fibre, plenty of water and movement or exercise are some of the keys to avoiding constipation, but here are some specific remedies that can be especially helpful.

Castor Oil Drink

1 tbsp castor oil
1 glass hot water OR fruit juice

1 Mix the castor oil with the water or juice to help mask the taste.

2 Drink in one go.

CAUTION

Do not use this if you are pregnant or have an intestinal obstruction

FREQUENCY

Once a day for up to 3 days. Do not use as a long-term treatment as this could cause side effects like cramping and diarrhoea. Use every 2-3 months at most

NOTE

It is usually effective within 2-6 hours so don't take it at bedtime.

After castor oil is consumed, it releases ricinoleic acid, a type of unsaturated fatty acid with a laxative effect. Ricinoleic acid works by binding to receptors in the intestinal walls, causing the intestinal muscles to contract and push out stool – just as other stimulant laxatives work. Research has found castor oil to alleviate constipation symptoms, such as straining and hard, dry stools.

Pranayama (Kapalbhati)

This is also effective for gassiness and bloating.

1 Sit upright, close your eyes and take a deep breath in.

2 Expel the breath with many rapid, forceful contractions of the abdominal muscles until all breath has been exhaled.

3 Then take a deep breath and exhale slowly.

4 Repeat this process for 10 minutes.

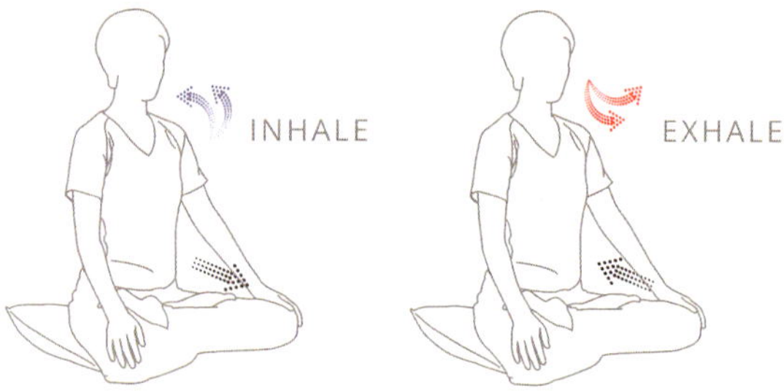

NOTE

Do not do this within an hour after eating.

CAUTION

Do not do this if you are pregnant, recently had abdominal surgery, have a slipped disc, pacemaker or stent, hernia or high blood pressure

FREQUENCY

Daily

> Kapalbhati can encourage bowel movements as it stimulates abdominal muscles through rapid contractions, therefore helping the stool pass through quicker. Furthermore, by reducing the intestinal transit time, the body absorbs less water from the stool. This prevents the stool from getting too hard and dry, thus making it easier to pass.

Bedtime Ghee

1-2 tsp ghee
1 cup warm milk OR water
½ tsp honey (optional – adjust to taste)

1 Mix the ghee and honey (if using) in a cup of warm milk or water.

2 Drink this before bed.

FREQUENCY

Every night if needed

Ghee contains butyric acid, a short-chain fatty acid with anti-inflammatory effects that has been found to help with digestion, reduce pain when passing stool, and reduce incidences of constipation.

Consuming warm liquid can widen blood vessels in the digestive system, helping to increase blood flow, which strengthens muscle contractions in the GI tract, helping the stool to pass through more quickly.

Prunes & Figs

4 prunes
2 figs

1 Eat the above quantity of prunes and figs daily.

Prunes have a high fibre content, of which the insoluble fibre adds bulk to the stool, helping it to move through the intestines faster, and the soluble fibre soaks up water which softens the stool. Prunes also contain sorbitol, which draws water into the intestines, helping to induce bowel movements. Research has found prunes can improve stool frequency and consistency better than laxatives like psyllium.

Figs similarly have high fibre content, and studies have found them to speed up intestinal transit time, improve stool consistency, and alleviate stomach discomfort associated with constipation.

Diarrhoea

Green Bananas

You can consume these in a smoothie, or by baking or by boiling them. Generally, cooking the bananas can help to ensure you don't feel bloated or gassy. You can eat them as a snack or as a side with your meal.

If boiling:

1. Without peeling, cut off both ends of each banana.
2. Make a slit along the side, without cutting into the flesh.
3. Add the bananas to boiling salted water and cook until tender – about 20 minutes.

Add a little oil to the water – the dark bits will rise to the top so you can scoop them out and discard.

4. Drain the water, remove the skin and serve.

If baking:

1. Cut each banana in half lengthways, keeping the skin on.
2. Place them on a baking tray with the skin-side down
3. Sprinkle a little bit of salt and olive oil on the flesh side of the bananas.
4. Bake in the oven on 180°C for around 30-40 minutes, then serve.

CAUTION

Do not consume if you have a latex-fruit allergy

Green bananas have been found to reduce the amount, severity and duration of episodes of diarrhoea. Green bananas' antidiarrheal effects are partly due to the resistant starch and pectin they contain. Resistant starch and pectin can't be digested, so it stimulates the bowels to absorb more water and firm up the stool. Bananas are also rich in potassium (an important mineral and electrolyte), which is often lost through diarrhoea and therefore needs replenishing.

Lime Water

2 cups water
2 tbsp fresh lime or lemon juice (this will take approx. 1 lime or ½ lemon)
2 tsp sugar
¼ tsp rock salt
Mint leaves (optional – for garnish)

1. Mix together all the ingredients until well combined.
2. Taste and adjust the sweet, savoury or tangy flavours to your liking. You can also add more water to dilute it.
3. Garnish with mint and drink.

FREQUENCY

No more than 6 cups a day

NOTE

Rinse your mouth with plain water afterwards to prevent the citric acid from eroding your tooth enamel.

This drink is typically served cold, but you can use warm water if you prefer.

Diarrhoea causes a loss of fluids and electrolytes (minerals that your body needs to function). Therefore, drinking water is important to replace these and avoid dehydration.

Consuming sugar and salt with water helps the intestines to absorb fluids more efficiently, as the salt slows down fluid loss and the sugar helps the body absorb the salt. Salt and sugar solutions have been found to rehydrate the body more effectively after diarrhoea than water alone.

Lime (and lemon) juice has antimicrobial properties, and has been found to inhibit pathogens that commonly cause diarrhoea and vomiting, such as norovirus and *E. coli*. Limes are also high in antioxidants, which can help to combat the oxidative stress associated with chronic diarrhoea.

Cumin Buttermilk

1 cup probiotic/live yoghurt
1 cup water
½ tsp ground cumin
¼ tsp salt (adjust to taste)
Coriander leaves, finely chopped (for garnish)

1. Add all the ingredients except the coriander to a blender (if you don't have a blender, you can use a whisk and a large bowl).
2. Blend or whisk until everything is combined and lightly frothy. If needed you can add more water to make it runnier.
3. Pour into a glass, top with the chopped coriander, and drink.

FREQUENCY

As often as you like

NOTE

If you're taking antibiotics, make sure to wait a couple of hours after a dose before drinking this.

> Research has found cumin to have antimicrobial properties that can reduce the risk of foodborne illnesses including *E. coli*. Cumin has also been found to be effective at reducing frequency of diarrhoea in patients with IBS.

Coriander contains antimicrobial compounds, such as dodecanal, which has been shown to help fight infections and foodborne illnesses, like *Salmonella*, which may be causing diarrhoea.

Yoghurt contains probiotics, which are 'good' bacteria that support healthy gut function and protect it against infection. Research has found that probiotics significantly reduce the duration of diarrhoea. This could be because they help to restore the balance of bacteria when the digestive system is changed by antibiotics, bacterial infections or viruses – all of which are potential causes of diarrhoea.

White Rice & Yoghurt

For lunch and dinner, just eat a bowl of white rice with some yoghurt. Make sure the yoghurt you get says live, active or probiotic on it.

If you want some variety, you can swap out the white rice for tapioca pearls and cook it as follows:

1. Rinse and drain the tapioca pearls.
2. Put the tapioca in a bowl and pour in just enough water to cover them.
3. Leave to soak for 4 hours or overnight.
4. Check that they are soft enough by pressing them between your fingers – if they are done then they will be soft and get mashed easily, otherwise soak for longer.
5. Drain any remaining water.
6. Warm the tapioca in a non-stick pan on low heat for 2-3 minutes until it turns almost transparent. Sprinkle some salt while it cooks.

OPTIONAL

You can add a pinch of cumin seeds when you heat it, or add some ground cumin to the yoghurt you eat with it.

NOTE

If you're taking antibiotics, make sure to wait a couple of hours after a dose before eating yoghurt.

Yoghurt contains probiotics, which are 'good' bacteria that support healthy gut function and protect it against infection. Research has found that probiotics significantly reduce the duration of diarrhoea. This could be because they help to restore the balance of bacteria when the digestive system is changed by antibiotics, bacterial infections or viruses – all of which are potential causes of diarrhoea.

White rice and tapioca are both starchy and low-fibre, which means they have a binding effect in the digestive tract, resulting in firmer, bulkier stools. They are also bland, which helps to minimise the risk of further stomach irritation.

Gassiness & Bloating

Cumin Seed Paste

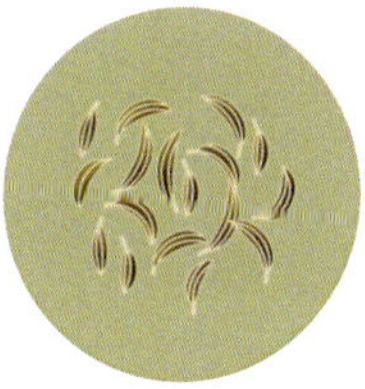

½ tsp cumin seeds

1 Chew the cumin seeds until they become a paste in your mouth.

2 Then swallow.

FREQUENCY

As often as needed, either after meals or at the first signs of gas and bloating

Adding cumin seeds to your meals can also be effective.

Cumin is a carminative spice, meaning it can reduce bloating and flatulence. Whilst the mechanism for how cumin reduces gas and bloating is unclear, numerous studies have shown cumin to be an effective treatment for it, including bloating associated with irritable bowel syndrome (IBS).

Baking Soda Soak

This is to use if cooking beans, lentils or peas.

½ tsp baking soda/bicarbonate of soda (per litre of water)
Water

1. Cover the beans, peas or lentils with water in a pan or bowl.
2. Add the baking soda.
3. Leave to soak for at least a few hours.
4. Drain the water and use fresh water to cook.

Beans, peas and lentils contain particular carbohydrates known as FODMAPs, which are fermented by gut bacteria in the colon, and a by-product of this process is gas. Soaking these foods in water then discarding the water leaches out these carbohydrates that are responsible for gas production. Bicarbonate of soda has been found to significantly reduce the raffinose (a starch which is poorly digested, causing gassiness) content of peas, beans and lentils.

Ginger Tea

1 inch fresh ginger, thinly sliced
1-2 cups water

1. Bring the water to a boil in a saucepan.
2. Add the sliced ginger to the saucepan.
3. Simmer for 5 minutes on low heat. You can leave it for longer for stronger tea.
4. Pour the tea through a sieve to strain out the ginger.
5. Drink the tea just before a big meal, or at the first sign of bloating.

FREQUENCY

Up to 3 times a day

You can add some honey after straining out the ginger to sweeten the taste.

Ginger acts as a natural carminative (an agent that relieves flatulence), and can help to speed up gastric emptying and aid digestion by stimulating digestive juices including bile, therefore helping to reduce gas and bloating.

Yoga (Apanasana or Pawanmuktasana)

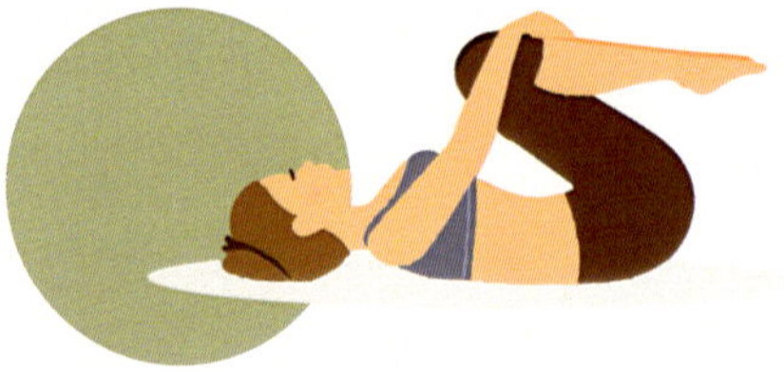

1 Lie on your back with your hands and legs relaxed.

2 Inhale, then as you exhale, bring your knees to your chest.

3 Clasp your hands around your knees and squeeze your knees in close to your chest so you feel some pressure on your abdomen. Make sure your back stays flat on the floor.

4 Hold this position for 5-10 deep breaths, then release your knees on the last exhale.

5 Repeat this process a few times or until you feel relief.

FREQUENCY

Daily but not within an hour after eating

NOTE

You can vary this pose by bringing one knee up at a time for 5-10 breaths. You can also bring your head up on the exhales so your forehead almost touches your knees.

> Yoga relaxes your body and releases tension. Relaxing your intestines whilst applying gentle pressure can help to pass gas and relieve bloating. Studies have found yoga to be effective at relieving bloating, along with other IBS symptoms.

Heartburn

Milk

Drink 3 to 4 sips of low-fat or skimmed cow's milk after eating a meal.

FREQUENCY

As often as needed

The calcium in milk has an acid-neutralising effect and can strengthen the LOS (the muscular ring that usually prevents stomach acid coming up into the oesophagus). The protein in milk stimulates gastrin secretion – a hormone which also strengthens LOS contraction and promotes the emptying of your stomach, meaning there are less contents to move back up and less time for acid reflux to occur.

Asafoetida Paste

½ tsp asafoetida
1-2 tsp ghee OR honey

1 Mix together the asafoetida and ghee (or honey).

2 Eat this before meals or at the first signs of acid reflux symptoms.

FREQUENCY

3 times a day before meals or as needed

Studies have found asafoetida relieve indigestion by increasing the activity of digestive enzymes, specifically by increasing the release of bile from the liver, which is needed for the digestion of fat. This is important as the longer that fatty foods sit in your digestive system, the more stomach acid gets produced, which can then worsen heartburn or acid reflux. Fats may also relax the LOS (the muscle that acts as a barrier between the oesophagus and stomach), meaning that stomach acid can escape into the oesophagus and cause heartburn.

The viscous nature of honey or ghee can provide relief by coating the mucous membrane of the oesophagus.

Aloe & Wheatgrass Shot

2 tbsp aloe vera juice
1 tbsp wheatgrass juice OR ¼-½ tsp wheatgrass powder

1 Mix together the aloe vera and wheatgrass.

2 Drink just before your meal.

CAUTION

Do not consume this if you are pregnant, or allergic to wheat or grass

FREQUENCY

Before any meals you tend to get heartburn or acid reflux after

You can add a little water if needed, or mix it into fruit juice to help with the taste.

Studies have found that GORD symptoms, like heartburn and acid reflux, may be due to inflammation and oxidative stress, rather than just chemical injury from stomach acid. Aloe vera contains powerful antioxidants, and has anti-inflammatory properties, which can therefore help to reduce these symptoms. Research has in fact found aloe vera juice to be as effective as common medications (including proton pump inhibitors and H2 blockers) for reducing acid reflux symptoms, without the negative side effects.

Similarly, wheatgrass is anti-inflammatory, and is rich in antioxidants (vitamins A, C, E) and vitamin B – both of which have been shown to reduce acid reflux or GORD symptoms. Wheatgrass also contains high levels of digestive enzymes that can help to break down food quicker. This means that food moves through the stomach faster, leaving less contents and time for acid reflux to occur.

Cumin Seed Paste

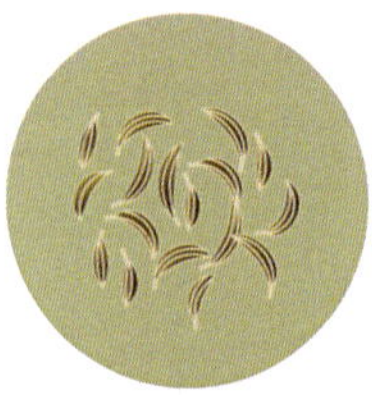

½ tsp cumin seeds

1 Chew the cumin seeds until they become a paste in your mouth.
2 Then swallow.

FREQUENCY

As often as needed, either after meals or at the first signs of heartburn

Adding cumin seeds to your meals can also be effective.

Cumin helps to address acid reflux and heartburn by increasing the activity of digestive enzymes and release of bile from the liver, therefore speeding up digestion. As the food is moved through the stomach faster, it leaves less contents and time for acid reflux to occur.

Liquorice Tea

1 inch liquorice root
2 cups water

1. Bring the water to a boil in a saucepan.
2. Add the piece of liquorice root and simmer on low heat for a few minutes.
3. Strain into a cup and drink.

CAUTION

Do not consume if you are pregnant, have high blood pressure or low potassium

FREQUENCY

Up to twice daily for no more than 4 weeks

SHORTCUT

You can buy liquorice teabags and make it as you would any other herbal tea.

You can make extra and refrigerate it so you don't have to boil it every time.

> Research has found that liquorice increases the mucus coating of the oesophageal lining, which may act as a barrier to the irritating effects of stomach acid. This barrier can also allow any damaged or irritated oesophageal tissue to heal.

Yoga (Vajrasana)

1. Kneel on the floor or a mat with the soles of your feet facing up. Make sure your knees and ankles are together and your feet are flat on the ground.
2. Sit back on your legs so your bottom rests on your heels.
3. Place your hands on your thighs with your arms relaxed, and adjust your pelvis back and forth until you feel comfortable.
4. Sit straight so your spine is lengthened, look straight ahead, and take deep breaths.
5. Continue for at least 30 seconds, or as long as you feel comfortable holding the pose.

FREQUENCY

After every meal. As you do it more often, try to gradually increase the amount of time you hold the pose for up to 20-30 minutes at most

If you have ankle pain, place a folded blanket or pillow under your shins and feet so your toes hang off the back. For knee pain, tuck the blanket or pillow behind your knees.

This pose restricts blood flow to the legs, increasing blood flow to the abdominal area, which helps to speed up digestion. As the food is moved through the stomach faster, it allows less time for acid reflux to occur and less contents to come back up. Additionally, stress often triggers heartburn and acid reflux symptoms; yoga is proven to reduce stress and has specifically been shown to relieve symptoms of GORD (a chronic, more severe form of acid reflux) such as heartburn.

Stomach Ache Or Pain

Common causes of stomach aches or pain tend to be indigestion, bloating, constipation, diarrhoea and so on, so see those sections for remedies (pages 164-184). If you're not sure of the cause, or want general relief, continue reading for some all-rounder remedies you can try.

Note that you should see a doctor if the stomach pain is so severe you can't function properly, or is accompanied by bloody stools, difficulty breathing, weight loss, diarrhoea for more than a few days, fever or vomiting, or the stomach is painful to touch.

Cumin, Coriander & Fennel Tea

½ tsp cumin seeds
½ tsp coriander seeds
½ tsp fennel seeds
2 cups water

1. Bring the water to a boil in a saucepan.
2. Add all the seeds and simmer on low heat for 5-10 minutes.
3. Strain out the seeds and drink.

FREQUENCY

As often as needed. If you frequently get stomach aches, drink this daily

You can add a pinch of cinnamon powder if you prefer a slightly sweeter flavour.

Cumin helps to address stomach pain caused by indigestion by increasing the activity of digestive enzymes and release of bile from the liver, therefore speeding up digestion. Cumin also has antimicrobial properties that can reduce the risk of foodborne infections. More notably, cumin has been found so effective at treating cramps, digestive spasms and bloating associated with IBS, that researchers believe it to be an effective replacement for those who can't afford expensive medications to treat IBS.

Fennel seeds can reduce stomach pain by soothing swelling and irritation in the intestines due to its anti-inflammatory properties, which mainly come from the component anethole. Soothing muscles in the intestines can also help to relieve gassiness – a common cause of stomach pain.

Coriander has been found to significantly decrease abdominal pain, bloating and discomfort in patients with IBS. Coriander also reduces indigestion if regularly consumed, and contains antimicrobial compounds, such as dodecanal, which has been shown to fight foodborne illnesses, like *Salmonella*, which may be causing stomach ache.

Pressure Points

Navel Area

1 To find the pressure point, go two finger-widths below the belly button (see picture below).

2 Place one or two fingers on this pressure point.

3 Using gentle pressure, you can either massage this point in a circular motion or hold for five seconds then release.

4 Massage for 2-3 minutes or repeat holding pressure 3 times.

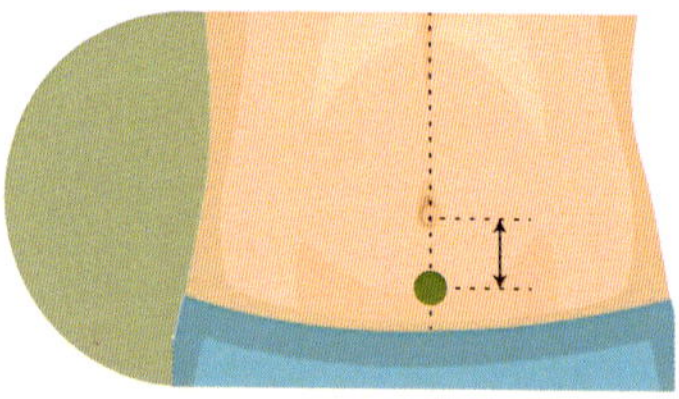

Base of Thumb

1 Press firmly with your thumb on the pressure point shown below on the other hand.

2 Hold for five seconds then release.

3 Repeat three times on this hand, then do the same for the other hand.

FREQUENCY

As often as needed, unless the area becomes sore to touch

NOTE

You can also use this technique to directly massage the area that is in pain.

Apply an essential oil like lavender, as the scent can help reduce stress which may also be contributing to stomach pain.

Research has found acupressure to be effective at relieving general stomach pain, as well as improving bowel function and common causes of pain like gas and constipation. It is thought that applying pressure on certain points relieves pain by closing or blocking off nerve impulses that transmit pain to the brain. It can also signal to the brain to release pain-reducing chemicals into the bloodstream.

Urinary Tract Infections (UTIs)

Whilst severe UTIs or bladder infections might only be successfully treated with antibiotics, research suggests that mild UTIs can be resolved naturally, without the use of antibiotics. Moreover, if you have recurrent UTIs, natural remedies are a good solution to avoid the negative effects of long-term antibiotic use.

Coriander, Cumin & Cinnamon Water

½ tsp cumin seeds
½ tsp coriander seeds
1-2 cinnamon sticks OR ¼-½ tsp ground cinnamon
3 cups water

1. Bring the water to a boil in a saucepan.
2. Add the seeds and cinnamon stick(s) and simmer on low heat for 5-10 minutes. If using ground cinnamon, add it after you remove from heat.
3. Strain out the seeds and drink it all within an hour or two.

FREQUENCY

Up to 3 times a day if dealing with an active infection.
Once a day if it's for prevention

NOTE

Make sure to maintain a regular intake of water regardless of how often you drink this – aim for 1.5-2 litres per day.

You can make this in bulk, keeping the same ratios, let it cool, and store it in the fridge. Make sure to drink it on the same day.

> Coriander, cinnamon and cumin have been found to fight bacteria responsible for UTIs, including antibiotic-resistant strains. Coriander also has a diuretic effect, meaning it will help the body urinate more, which will help to flush out the bacteria from the urinary tract. More frequent urination also helps reduce the amount of time bacteria are exposed to cells in the urinary tract, reducing the risk of them attaching and causing or worsening an infection. Drinking water similarly helps by diluting the urine and increasing the frequency of urination.

D-Mannose Powder

Dissolve the recommended amount of powder in a glass of water, then drink the mixture.

> D-mannose is a naturally-occurring sugar that inhibits the ability of *E. coli* bacteria (which causes around 90% of UTIs) to stick to urinary tract cells, making it easier for them to be flushed out. Research has found D-mannose to be successful in treating active UTIs, as well as preventing UTI recurrence as or more effectively than common antibiotics, and without the unpleasant side effects.

Urinary Incontinence

Pomegranate Juice

Drink 1-2 cups of unsweetened pomegranate juice daily. You can drink it by itself or add it to a smoothie. If you want to make fresh juice from the fruit itself then use the following recipe:

1-2 pomegranate(s)
Blender
Sieve or mesh strainer

1. Seed the pomegranate.
2. Put the pomegranate seeds in a blender.
3. Pulse the seeds a few times in the blender to break them apart and release the juice. Don't overblend or seeds will break down.
4. Strain the juice using a sieve or mesh strainer.

You can use the back of a spoon to gently push against the pomegranate pulp to extract as much juice as possible.

6. If the juice feels too thick, you can add a little water.
7. Drink at room temperature or chill beforehand.

NOTE

You can store this in an airtight container in the fridge for about 2 days.

> Oxidative stress has been shown to be a cause of bladder dysfunction, including incontinence. Pomegranate is rich in antioxidants, mainly punicalagins, and can therefore reduce oxidative stress. Pomegranate has also been found to improve the levels of nitric oxide (NO) – low NO has been linked to bladder overactivity among other urological disorders, and it helps with smooth muscle relaxation i.e. it helps to stop involuntary contractions that bring on the urge to urinate.

Cinnamon Compress

1-2 tsp ground cinnamon
Water
1 piece of cloth/gauze
Surgical or medical tape (optional)

1 Mix the cinnamon with some water to make a paste.
2 Apply the paste to clean skin over the bladder region – between the belly button and pubic area.
3 Press the cloth onto the skin where the paste has been applied.
4 Hold it there or secure with tape for 2-4 hours.
5 Remove the cloth and wash or wipe off the paste.

FREQUENCY

Every other day

NOTE

Patch test the paste before using to make sure there is no skin irritation.

Recent research has shown cinnamon to effectively reduce symptoms of overactive bladder in both men and women when applied as a patch, and a lower severity of urgency was reported. Cinnamon is rich in the compound cinnamaldehyde, which has been found to significantly reverse signs of stress urinary incontinence by increasing the contractile force of the urethra (which helps to stop the unwanted flow of urine from the bladder).

Pumpkin Seeds

Eat a handful of pumpkin seeds every day. You can eat them on their own, add them to smoothies, yoghurt, fruit, salads, soups or even in your baking.

Pumpkin seeds can reduce the bioavailability of other nutrients you eat as they contain phytic acid, so you may want to soak them to reduce their phytic acid content.

NOTE

This may also help with urinary retention in men, as pumpkin seeds can address prostate enlargement (BPH) – a common cause of both urinary retention and incontinence in men – possibly by inhibiting 5-alpha reductase, which is how medications commonly used to relieve urinary retention symptoms associated with prostate enlargement work.

> Research has found pumpkin seeds to reduce symptoms of overactive bladder, significantly reducing both stress and urge incontinence and improving abnormal urinary function in both men and women. It's proposed that pumpkin seeds work by strengthening pelvic floor muscles (by inhibiting certain enzymes like aromatase) and have a direct muscle relaxing effect. This helps to prevent the involuntary contractions of bladder muscles, which is what pushes urine out.

Vomiting & Nausea

If you have just vomited, you should wait a few hours before using any oral remedies e.g. food or drink.

Ginger Tea

1 inch fresh ginger, thinly sliced
1-2 cups water

1 Bring the water to a boil in a saucepan.
2 Add the sliced ginger to the saucepan.
3 Simmer for 5 minutes on low heat. You can leave it for longer for stronger tea
4 Pour the tea through a sieve to strain out the ginger.
5 Drink the tea slowly – sip, don't gulp.

NOTE

You can alternatively chew on a small piece of fresh ginger.

FREQUENCY

Up to 3 times daily

Ginger contains gingerols and shogaols, which block the actions of neurotransmitters acetylcholine (which triggers involuntary stomach contractions), and serotonin (which can trigger the vomiting reflex). These mechanisms are how many anti-nausea medications work, and research has shown ginger to be as effective as some of these medications with fewer side effects. Ginger can also increase digestive responsiveness and speed stomach emptying, which can help reduce nausea.

Cumin Seed Paste

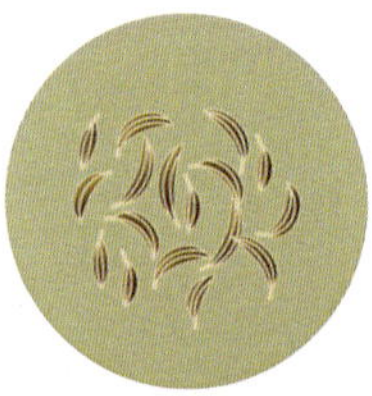

½ tsp cumin seeds

1 Chew the cumin seeds until they become a paste in your mouth.

2 Then swallow.

FREQUENCY

Up to 3 times daily

Research has found cumin to have antimicrobial properties that can reduce the risk of foodborne illnesses (including *E. coli* and *Salmonella*) – a common cause of vomiting. Cumin has also been found to be effective at reducing both mild and moderate nausea in individuals with IBS.

Lime Water

See page 169-170 for recipe and explanation.

Aromatherapy

5-8 cardamom pods OR 1 lemon OR small piece of fresh ginger
1 small container or jar with a lid

1. Release the aroma of your chosen ingredient:
   - Crush the cardamom pods
   - Freshly slice or zest the lemon
   - Peel and chop the fresh ginger
2. Put it in the small container or jar.
3. Open the jar, inhale the smell for 2 or 3 deep breaths or for 10-15 seconds, then close the jar.
4. Wait for 5 minutes then open the jar and smell again. If the smell fades too soon, repeat step 1 with fresh ingredients.

NOTE

If the ingredient you picked didn't help or made symptoms worse, try a different one as individuals respond to various scents differently.

You can alternatively use the essential oils of these ingredients – either by inhaling them, putting them in a diffuser or applying topically to your skin. You can even massage the oil onto your skin where the pressure points are located (see next page), but make sure to dilute it a little with a carrier oil like coconut oil.

FREQUENCY

As often as needed

Cardamom was found in a clinical trial to effectively reduce post-operative nausea. Another clinical trial found lemon inhalation aromatherapy to significantly reduce nausea and vomiting in pregnant women. Ginger aromatherapy has been found to reduce the occurrence and severity of nausea. A theory of how aromatherapy works is that the nasal receptor cells send impulses to the olfactory region of the brain, leading to the release of certain hormones or chemicals, which then cause physical and/or mental changes, such as reducing nausea or its causes like anxiety.

Pressure Point

1. Have your hand open with your palm facing up.
2. Count three finger-widths down from your wrist crease.
3. Press down with your thumb between the two tendons in this location.
4. Massage this point in a circular or up-and-down motion for 30-60 seconds.
5. Repeat on the other arm.

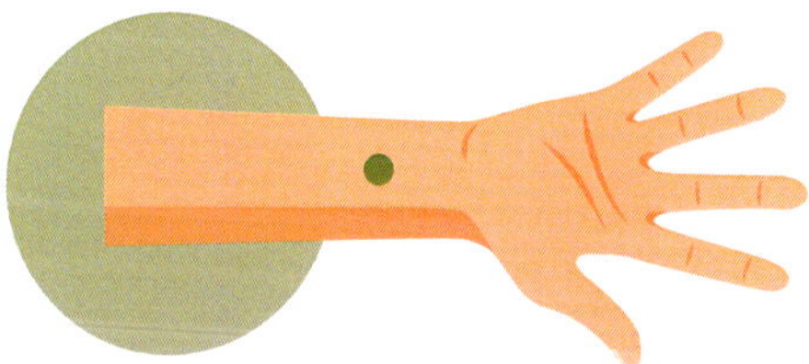

FREQUENCY

As often as needed

Applying pressure to certain points stimulates nerve fibres, which transmit signals to the brain and spinal cord, and these signals are thought to have the ability to decrease nausea. Studies have found acupressure to be as effective as anti-nausea medications at relieving symptoms, with almost no side effects. It has also been found to reduce the risk and severity of nausea after operations and chemotherapy.

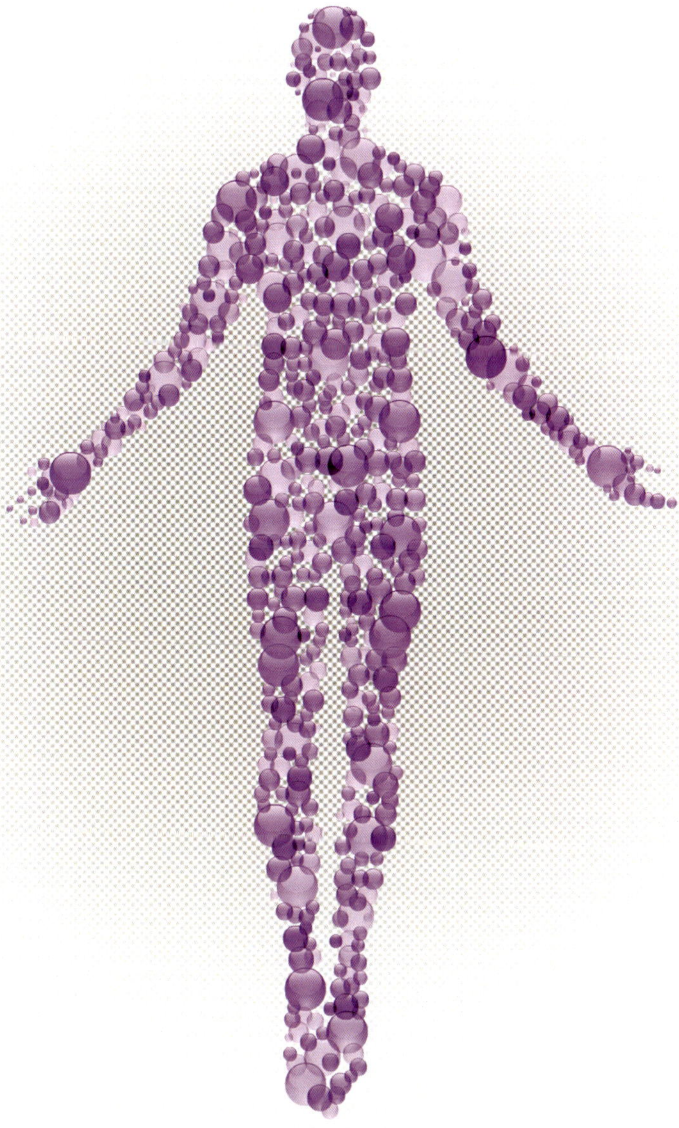

Miscellaneous

Miscellaneous Remedies

PAGE 202 Fatigue

PAGE 206 Headaches & Migraines

PAGE 208 Insect Bites

PAGE 211 Insomnia

PAGE 217 Loss of Appetite

PAGE 220 Menstrual Cramps (Dysmenorrhoea)

Fatigue

Pranayama (Kapalbhati)

1 Sit upright, close your eyes and take a deep breath in.
2 Expel the breath with many rapid, forceful contractions of the abdominal muscles until all breath has been exhaled.
3 Then take a deep breath and exhale slowly.
4 Repeat this process for 10 minutes.

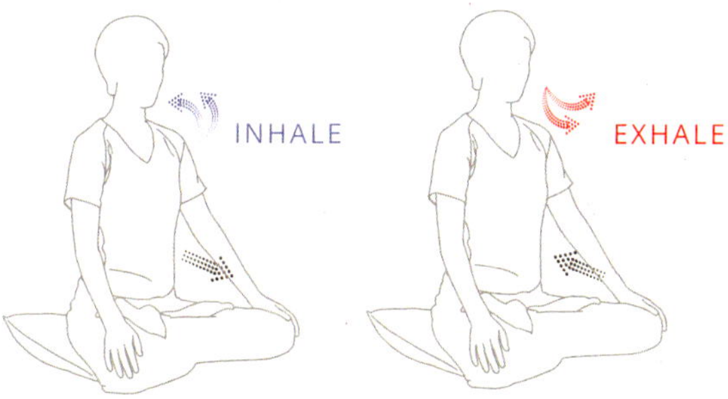

CAUTION

Do not do this if you are pregnant, recently had abdominal surgery, have a slipped disc, pacemaker or stent, hernia or high blood pressure

FREQUENCY

Daily

NOTE

Do not do this within an hour after eating.

> Studies have found that pranayama can improve symptoms of chronic fatigue syndrome (CFS) and increase resistance to anxiety and stress – a possible cause of fatigue. The rapid breathing in kapalbhati can help force out the air build-up in lungs and expel CO2, therefore increasing oxygen saturation and boosting energy.

Spiced Honey

1 tbsp ground turmeric
2 tsp ground cinnamon
½ tsp black pepper
4 tbsp honey

1. Mix together all the ingredients.
2. Consume ½ tablespoon of this mixture daily when you usually feel most tired e.g. mid-afternoon.

NOTE

You can make a larger quantity and store in the fridge for up to 1 week.

There are lots of ways to consume this – by itself, in a glass of warm water, in a smoothie, spread on toast, in yoghurt and so on.

Turmeric has been found to effectively reduce chronic fatigue and exercise-induced fatigue, as well as alleviating depression – one of the top causes of fatigue. This could be because turmeric's compounds, such as curcumin, help to regulate serotonin and dopamine levels (which are linked to mood and energy levels), or because curcumin blocks two proteins linked to severity of chronic fatigue syndrome.

Black pepper increases the bioavailability of curcumin in turmeric by up to 2000% i.e. improves the absorption of curcumin.

Cinnamon can improve sensitivity to insulin – one of the key hormones that regulate metabolism and energy use. Cinnamon also mimics insulin, which increases glucose transport to the cells, thus providing more energy, whilst lowering blood sugar by decreasing the amount of glucose in the bloodstream.

Honey's glucose content is absorbed quickly, providing an immediate energy boost, whilst the sustained energy comes from the fructose which is absorbed more slowly.

Lime Water

2 cups water
2 tbsp fresh lime or lemon juice
(this will take approx. 1 lime or ½ lemon)
2 tsp sugar
¼ tsp rock salt
Mint leaves (optional)

1. Mix together all the ingredients until well combined.
2. Taste it and adjust the sweet, savoury or tangy flavours to your liking. You can also add more water to dilute it.
3. Garnish with mint and drink in the morning or the time of day you feel most tired.

FREQUENCY

No more than 6 cups a day

NOTE

Rinse your mouth with plain water afterwards to prevent the citric acid from eroding your tooth enamel.

Limes and lemons are rich in citric acid and vitamin C, which have been found to significantly improve iron absorption from plant foods, and can therefore help to protect against iron deficiency anaemia – a common cause of fatigue.

Fatigue can also be caused by dehydration and loss of electrolytes (minerals that your body needs to function). Water itself helps to rehydrate and boost energy, and consuming sugar and salt with water helps the intestines to absorb fluids more efficiently. This is because the salt helps to retain fluid whilst restoring sodium levels (an electrolyte), and the sugar helps the body absorb electrolytes like sodium.

Headaches & Migraines

Clove & Lavender Massage

2 drops clove oil OR ¼ tsp ground cloves
2 drops lavender oil
1-2 tsp ghee OR carrier oil
(e.g. coconut oil, jojoba oil)

1. Mix together the clove oil (or cloves), lavender oil and ghee (or carrier oil).
2. Dip your fingertips in the mixture, and slowly massage your temples in circular motions, whilst applying a small amount of pressure.
3. Using the same circular motions, continue to massage the rest of your forehead, focusing on the areas you feel pain or tension.
4. Continue for about 10 minutes, or until you feel some relief.

Cloves are used topically for various types of pain, including headaches and migraines, due to the anti-inflammatory, analgesic compounds it contains – specifically eugenol. This helps to block or reduce the pain from the headache.

Inhaling the scent of lavender oil has been found to significantly reduce migraine and headache symptoms quickly, likely by calming the nervous system and reducing possible causes like stress and anxiety. Research has also found that applying lavender oil topically provides pain relief equivalent to that of tramadol, possibly due to lavender oil's anti-inflammatory, analgesic properties.

> Head massages have been found to reduce the frequency, duration and intensity of chronic tension headaches, as massaging can relieve tight or contracting muscles causing the headache.

Ginger Tea

1 inch fresh ginger, thinly sliced
1-2 cups water

1. Bring the water to a boil in a saucepan.
2. Add the sliced ginger to the saucepan.
3. Simmer for 5 minutes on low heat. You can leave it for longer for stronger tea.
4. Pour the tea through a sieve to strain out the ginger.
5. Drink the tea.

FREQUENCY

Up to 3 times daily

> Ginger's chemical compounds – including gingerols and shogaols – have anti-inflammatory and pain-relieving effects. Ginger may also increase serotonin, helping to reduce inflammation and restrict blood vessels; this is similar to how triptans (migraine medications) work. Studies show ginger to be effective at treating headaches and migraines, and alleviate migraines as effectively as the prescription drug sumatriptan. Ginger also reduces levels of prostaglandins – hormones linked to headaches and migraines – similar to how medicines like ibuprofen and aspirin work.

Insect Bites

Turmeric Paste

Ground turmeric
Water

1 Combine a small amount of the ground turmeric with a few drops of water to make a paste.
2 Apply it on the bite(s).
3 Rinse off after 15-20 minutes.

FREQUENCY

As often as needed

An insect bite prompts your body to release histamine as part of an inflammatory response, which causes itching and swelling around the bite. Turmeric can ease this as it contains curcumin, which has potent anti-inflammatory and antioxidant properties, thus helping to reduce swelling and soothe itching.

Essential Oils Ointment

15 drops lavender OR tea tree oil
1-2 tbsp coconut oil OR water

1. Dilute the drops of lavender or tea tree oil with water or coconut oil.
2. Apply directly to the bite(s).

FREQUENCY

Up to 3 times a day

NOTE

Store any leftover mixture in an airtight container in a cool, dry place.

Both lavender and tea tree oil have soothing and pain-relieving properties. Both have been found to have notable anti-inflammatory effects, reducing histamine release, which can therefore help with swelling and itching caused by the bite. They are also antimicrobial, which can help prevent an infection from the bite. Both can provide relief for all bites such as from mosquitoes and ticks, but lavender oil is especially helpful for spider bites, fire ant bites and bee stings.

Coconut oil has anti-inflammatory and antimicrobial properties which, like lavender and tea tree oil, can help reduce swelling and itching from the bite, as well as help prevent an infection. The oil also forms a thin layer over the bite which protects from any dust or dirt that might irritate it or cause infection.

Soothing Aloe Vera Gel

Fresh aloe vera OR
store-bought organic aloe vera gel

1 Apply aloe vera gel to the bite(s).

2 Let it dry.

FREQUENCY

As often as needed

Put in the fridge before use for a more soothing, cooling sensation.

Aloe vera gel has been shown to have anti-inflammatory properties, which reduce swelling and inflammation caused by the bite, therefore reducing the itch. It also has powerful antibacterial, antiseptic and analgesic properties due to the presence of certain compounds called anthraquinones. Aloe vera's moisturising effects further help to reduce and prevent itching, as dry skin around the bite can worsen the itching.

Insomnia

Saffron Milk

1-2 cups milk (for dairy-free, use almond or coconut milk)
1 pinch saffron threads (a 'pinch' is about 20 threads)

1. Warm the milk in a pan or microwave, then add the saffron threads.
    - If warming in a pan, keep it on low heat for 2-3 minutes after adding the saffron – do not boil!
    - If warming in the microwave, add the saffron threads after warming the milk, and leave it to soak for 5-10 minutes.
2. Pour into a mug and drink before bed.

FREQUENCY

Every night if needed

You can slightly squeeze the saffron threads to release some of their colour into the milk before drinking.

NOTE

This remedy can also be used for babies over the age of 6 months whilst travelling but make sure to use no more than 2 strands of saffron.

Saffron acts as mild sedative and research has shown it to help induce restorative sleep, even in low quantities, though the mechanism is unclear.

Studies indicate that warm milk can help induce sleep, possibly due to the psychological link to having good sleep as a child after drinking warm milk, or the calming effect of having a bedtime ritual – especially as warm beverages can alleviate anxiety and calm the nervous system. It could also be due to the presence of two compounds – tryptophan and melatonin – which are known to induce sleep and help with sleep disorders.

Poppy Seed Milk

2 tbsp poppy seeds
1-2 cups milk (for dairy-free, use almond or coconut milk)
1 tbsp honey (adjust to your taste)
5 pistachios, slivered or roughly chopped
5-10 saffron threads, soaked in 1 tsp of milk for 5 minutes before use (optional)
Water

1. Soak the poppy seeds in water for 6 hours or overnight. Then drain them and grind into a paste. Add a small amount of water if needed to grind.
2. In a saucepan, add the paste and honey to the milk.
3. Simmer on low heat for 10-15 minutes whilst stirring regularly. Make sure the paste is fully dissolved – the milk will feel thicker.
4. Pour this into a mug and top with the pistachios and saffron.
5. Drink before bed.

FREQUENCY

Every night if needed

Poppy seeds are rich in magnesium and calcium. Calcium helps the brain use tryptophan to make melatonin, which induces sleep. Magnesium supports deep, restorative sleep by increasing levels of GABA – a neurotransmitter that promotes sleep and encourages relaxation. Studies have also shown that even a small magnesium deficiency can lead to disturbed sleep.

Saffron acts as mild sedative and research has shown it to help induce restorative sleep, even in low quantities, though the mechanism is unclear.

Studies indicate that warm milk can help induce sleep, possibly due to the psychological link to having good sleep as a child after drinking warm milk, or the calming effect of having a bedtime ritual – especially as warm beverages can alleviate anxiety and calm the nervous system. It could also be due to the presence of two compounds – tryptophan and melatonin – which are known to induce sleep and help with sleep disorders.

Pistachios contain high doses of melatonin which helps induce restorative sleep. The nuts are also high in protein, which is associated with improved sleep quality, including less disturbed sleep.

Honey slightly raises insulin, releasing tryptophan, which helps make melatonin. Honey also restocks the liver's glycogen – this is important as the body often doesn't have enough glycogen supply for the whole night, so the brain tells the body it needs to eat, which then disturbs sleep.

Lavender Aromatherapy

This is a widely known remedy for sleep problems. All you need is some lavender essential oil, and there are a number of ways you can use it:

- Put a few drops of the oil on your pillow.
- Add some drops of the oil to a diffuser and place next to your bed.
- Dab a drop or two of the oil to your temples, wrist and/or neck before bed.
- Apply a few drops of the oil on the neckline or collar of your pyjamas.
- Add a few drops of the oil to your body lotion and use it before bed.

> Several studies have shown that the soothing fragrance of lavender oil calms the nervous system, and that inhaling the scent before sleep can improve sleep quality and duration, helping to increase deep, slow-wave sleep and reduce disturbances.

Nuts & Seeds

15-20 almonds
1-2 tsp fennel seeds

1. Grind the almonds and fennel seeds to a powder.
2. Consume this an hour before bed. You can have it by itself, in warm milk or water.

FREQUENCY

Every night if needed

Almonds contain high doses of melatonin, a hormone that helps regulate the sleeping cycle. Almonds also contain calcium and magnesium. Calcium helps the brain use tryptophan to make melatonin, which induces sleep. Magnesium supports deep, restorative sleep by increasing levels of GABA – a neurotransmitter that promotes sleep and encourages relaxation. Studies have also shown that even a small magnesium deficiency can lead to disturbed sleep.

Fennel seeds also have high magnesium content, and the seeds can relax muscle tension – a common cause of restlessness and difficulty falling asleep.

Pranayama (Anulom Vilom)

1. Take a deep breath in through your left nostril whilst closing your right nostril with your thumb.
2. Then, breathe in through your right nostril, hold, and exhale through your left nostril by closing your right nostril with your thumb.
3. Then, breathe in through your right nostril, hold, and exhale through your left nostril.

FREQUENCY

Repeat this process for 5-10 minutes every night

> The deep breathing involved in pranayama helps the mind and body relax as it replenishes oxygen in the body and reduces stress and anxiety. Clinical studies have also shown pranayama to quickly reduce heart rate as it activates the parasympathetic nervous system, making it easier to fall asleep.

Loss of Appetite

Loss of appetite can have a variety of underlying causes, so aside from the following remedies, it may be worth referring to other sections of the book, such as digestive, immune system, and metabolic problems.

Ginger & Coriander Water

1 inch fresh ginger, thinly sliced
OR 2 tsp dried ginger powder
½ tsp coriander seeds, crushed or powdered
1-2 cups of water

1. Bring the water to a boil in a saucepan.
2. Add the ginger and coriander seeds to the saucepan.
3. Simmer for 5 minutes on low heat.
4. Pour the tea through a sieve to strain out the ginger (if using fresh ginger) and coriander seeds.
5. Let it cool to room temperature or refrigerate it.
6. Drink 10 minutes before eating a meal.

FREQUENCY

Daily

You can make a larger quantity of this and store in the fridge for up to 3 days.

NOTE

You can alternatively chew a small piece of fresh ginger until you've got most of the juice out of it. Do this 15 minutes before eating a meal.

> Both ginger and coriander have been found to increase appetite when consumed as a beverage before eating; ginger and coriander are carminative, meaning they can relieve the 'heavy stomach' feeling from bloating and flatulence, therefore improving appetite. They can also stimulate fat digestion, which helps improve appetite as fat plays a key role in keeping you full due to it taking longer to digest. Ginger has also been found to increase ghrelin (a hormone that increases appetite by sending a signal to your brain to feel hungry) and reduce levels of leptin (a hormone that decreases appetite).

Herbs & Spices

Add carminative herbs and spices to your cooking, such as fennel seeds, black pepper, ginger, cinnamon, cardamom, cumin, and so on.

> Carminative herbs and spices have been found to improve appetite by relieving the 'heavy stomach' feeling from bloating and flatulence, and by stimulating bile production which facilitates fat digestion, therefore reducing the feeling of fullness. Moreover, herbs and spices can make meals more appealing; research has found that when food has a pleasant smell and taste, it can trigger appetite.

Bigger Plates

Use bigger plates when serving food to encourage yourself to eat larger portions.

> Studies have shown that people tend to fill their plates regardless of size, so taking a larger plate encourages an increase in serving size whilst feeling like it's a normal-sized portion. Research has found that this holds even when the food is unappealing.

Menstrual Cramps (Dysmenorrhea)

The following remedies can also ease symptoms of premenstrual syndrome (PMS) and heavy bleeding.

Turmeric & Cinnamon Ghee

1 tsp ground turmeric
½ tsp ground cinnamon
2 tsp ghee, melted
1 pinch black pepper

1. Mix together all the ingredients.
2. Consume the mixture, either by itself or in a cup of warm water.

FREQUENCY

Up to twice a day for as many days as needed

You can also warm this mixture in your hands or microwave and use it to massage your abdomen and sides. Add a few drops of lavender oil too for a more relaxing effect.

> Before and during menstruation, inflammatory prostaglandins are released as the uterine lining is shed, which triggers uterine muscle contractions, causing painful cramps. Higher levels of prostaglandins are associated with more severe cramps. Some of these prostaglandins can also enter the bloodstream, causing headache, nausea, vomiting, and diarrhoea.

Ghee's anti-inflammatory effects reduce the production of prostaglandins, possibly due to the conjugated linoleic acid (a type of fatty acid) it contains.

Turmeric contains curcumin, which has potent anti-inflammatory effects and has also been found to reduce prostaglandin levels. Research has shown curcumin to be effective in treating PMS symptoms.

Black pepper increases the bioavailability of curcumin i.e. increases its absorption.

Studies have shown cinnamon to reduce menstrual pain, heavy bleeding, as well as other PMS symptoms like nausea and vomiting. This is largely attributed to its compounds cinnamaldehyde, which has an antispasmodic effect, and eugenol, which reduces the production of prostaglandins.

Ginger & Black Pepper Tea

1 inch fresh ginger, thinly sliced
1 pinch black pepper
1-2 cups water

1. Bring the water to a boil in a saucepan.
2. Add the sliced ginger and black pepper to the saucepan.
3. Simmer for 5 minutes on low heat. You can leave it for longer for stronger tea.
4. Pour the tea through a sieve to strain out the ginger.

For added benefits, you can add ½ tsp turmeric and ½ tsp cinnamon to the tea.

> Ginger lowers levels of cramp-causing prostaglandins, and has been found to be as effective as non-steroidal anti-inflammatory drugs (NSAIDs) like ibuprofen for relieving menstrual pain. Ginger has also been shown to reduce heavy menstrual bleeding and the severity of PMS symptoms.

Saffron Milk

1-2 cups cow's milk (can be low or full fat) OR calcium-fortified milk alternative
10-13 saffron threads

If you want it warm/hot:

1. Warm the milk in a pan or microwave, then add the saffron threads.
    - If warming in a pan, keep it on low heat for 2-3 minutes after adding the saffron – do not boil!
    - If warming in the microwave, add the saffron threads after warming the milk, and leave it to soak for 5-10 minutes.
2. Pour into a mug and drink before bed.

If you want it cold:

1. Add the saffron threads to the mug of milk.
2. Leave to soak for 30 minutes.
3. Drink.

You can slightly squeeze the saffron threads to release some of their colour into the milk before drinking.

FREQUENCY

No more than 3 times a day

Saffron has been found effective at reducing PMS symptoms including pain, cramps, irritability, headaches and anxiety. This is thought to be because saffron helps correct a dysregulation of the serotonergic system (which is considered responsible for the majority of PMS symptoms) by inhibiting synaptic serotonin reuptake i.e. it keeps serotonin in the brain for longer.

Milk is one of the richest dietary sources of calcium, and several studies have found PMS patients to have an altered calcium balance, whilst calcium and milk intake have been found to improve symptoms of PMS, including pain.

Bibliography

As this book required reading and referencing an extensive amount of research papers, the references filled over 70 pages when written out. I know for myself I rarely read the bibliography, so to be kinder to the environment and save paper, you can see it online by scanning the QR code below or visiting **www.naturalremedylab.co.uk/research**.

You will be able to view the research used for a specific chapter or for the whole book.

Index

A

Aches, muscle, 124-29
Acid reflux. *See* Heartburn
Acne, 64-73
Acne scars, 105-8
Allergic rhinitis, 158-59
Allergies
  hay fever, 158-59
  itchy eyes, 8-10, 160
  runny or blocked nose, 26-28
Almond, 215
Almond oil, sweet, 71, 92, 94
Aloe vera, 71-2, 74-5, 84, 88, 104, 180, 210
Amla oil, 43
Angina, 14-18
Appetite, loss of, 217-9
Aromatherapy, for relieving
  difficulty sleeping, 214
  nausea, 196-97
Arteries, clogged, angina from, 14
Arthritis, 112-23
Asafoetida, 179
Asthma, 19-20
Astringent, 66, 70, 91, 97, 98-99
Atopic dermatitis,
  symptoms of dandruff, 36-39
  red or inflamed skin, 100-104.
    See also Eczema
Autoimmune disorders.
  See Immune system
Avocado, 87, 93, 136

B

Back pain. *See* Joint pain; Muscle pain
Bad breath, 48-50
Bags under the eyes, 90-92
Baking soda, 7, 175
Baldness. *See* Hair loss
Banana, 41-2, 57, 93, 136, 138, 168
Basil, 32-33
Bee stings. *See* Insect bites
Bites, insect, 208-10
Black pepper, 16-17, 20-22, 32-33, 52, 112-13, 125-26, 135, 139, 141-42, 150-51, 154-55, 158, 203, 218, 220-21
Blemishes, 64-73
Blepharitis, 8-10
Bloating, 174-77
Blood pressure, high, 31-33
Blood sugar, high, 140-42
Blueberries, 124
Breakouts. *See* Acne
Breathing
  for immune system, 156
  for relieving
    anxiety, 202, 216
    fatigue, 202
    high blood pressure, 32
    insomnia, 216
    joint or muscle pain, 118
  for thyroid disease, 146
Bruises, 81-84
Bug bites, 208-10
Burns, 74-78
Buttermilk, 36, 80, 90-91, 171

C

Calluses, 79-80
Camphor oil, 77-78, 126-27
Canker sores, 57-61
Cardamom, 16, 21, 138, 154-55, 196-97, 218
Carpal tunnel syndrome, 117-118. *See also* Joint pain
Carrot, 152-53
Castor oil, 79, 92, 164
Cayenne pepper, 115-16
Celery seed, 112, 114
Chalazia, 11
Chamomile, 58
Chapped lips, 85-89
Chest pain. *See* Angina; Heartburn
Chia seed, 116-17
Chickpeas, 139
Cholesterol, high, 15, 17-18, 143-45
Chronic fatigue syndrome (CFS), 202-3
Cinnamon, 16, 49, 70, 85, 97, 112, 125, 141-43, 150, 189, 192, 203, 220

Circles, dark, under the eyes, 90-92
Clove, 6, 53, 126-27, 150, 206
Coconut oil, 38-42, 44, 61, 81, 85, 88, 115, 159, 209
Coconut water, 125
Colds, 26-28
Compresses
for relieving
canker sores, 58
cuts or bruises, 81
dry, sore or irritated eyes, 9
joint pain or arthritis, 117
styes and chalazia, 11
toothache, 56
urinary incontinence, 192
Congestion, 26-28
from hay fever, 158-59
Conjunctivitis, 8-9, 11, 160
Constipation, 164-67
Coriander seed, 73, 185-86, 189-90, 217-18
Corns, 79-80
Coronary artery disease. *See* Angina
Coughing, 21-25
Cramps
abdominal, 185-88
menstrual, 220-23
muscle, 124-129
Crohn's disease. *See* Bloating; Constipation; Stomach cramps; Diarrhoea; Fatigue; Gassiness. *See also* Autoimmune disorders
Cucumber, 75-76
Cumin, 73, 150, 171, 174, 181, 185, 189, 195
Cuts, 81-84
scars from, 105-8
Cystitis. *See* Urinary tract infections (UTIs)
Cysts
on eye, 11
with acne, 64-73

D

Damaged hair, 40-41
Dandruff, 36-39
Dark chocolate, 144
Dark circles under the eyes, 90-92
Deep breathing. *See* Breathing
Dehydration
caused by diarrhoea, 169-70
fatigue from, 204-5
Dermatitis
atopic, 93-96
seborrheic, of scalp, 37, 39
Diabetes, 141-42
Diarrhoea, 168-73
Difficulty getting out of bed. *See* Fatigue
Dry
eyes, 8-10
hair, 40-41
lips, 85-89
skin, 93-96
Dysmenorrhoea. *See* Menstrual cramps

E

Earache, 6
Eardrops, 6-7
Ear infections, 6-7
Earwax, 7
Eczema, 93-96
Egg, 42, 99, 137
Enlarged pores, 97-99
Essential oils, for relieving
burns, 74-75
head lice, 44-45
headache, 206
insect bites, 209
insomnia, 214
muscle pain, 126-27
toothache, 53
Exercise
for overweight, 133
for underweight, 137
Exhaustion. *See* Fatigue; Insomnia
Eyedrops, 8, 10
Eyelid problems. *See* Chalazia
Eyes
bags under, 90-92
dark circles under, 90-92
dry, 8-10
infections of, 11

irritations of, 8-10
puffy, 90-92
sties on, 11
strain of, 9-10
Eye strain, 9-10

F

Fat, how to reduce, 132-35
Fatigue, 202-5
Fennel seed, 48, 73, 185-6, 215, 218
Fenugreek seed, 101-2, 112, 114, 134, 140
Figs, 167
Fine hair, 42-43
Flatulence. *See* Gassiness
Flax seed, 116-18, 143
Flu, symptoms of
congestion, 26-28
diarrhoea, 168-73
immune system, strengthening, 150-57
sore throat, 21-25
stomach cramps, 185-88
vomiting, 194-98
Foot problems
corns and calluses, 79-80
pain or stiffness, 112-29
Frizzy hair, 40-41

G

Garlic, 6-7, 15, 23-24, 26-27, 54, 72, 81-82, 112-13, 152-54
Gassiness, 174-77
Gastroesophageal reflux. *See* Heartburn
Ghee, 61, 85, 89, 166, 179, 206, 220-21
Ginger, 8, 16, 19, 21, 24, 27, 29, 81, 112, 115, 125, 141, 146, 152, 154, 176, 194, 196, 207, 217, 221
Gingivitis. *See* Gum infection
Gout, 114. *See* also Arthritis
Gram flour, 65-66
Green tea, 71, 102-3
Gum disease. *See* Gum infection
Gum infection, 51-52

H

Hair
coarse, 40-41
dandruff, 36-39
dry or damaged, 40-41
frizzy, 40-41
loss of, 42-43
Hair loss, 42-43
Halitosis. *See* Bad breath
Hands, dry. *See* Dry skin
Hand pain, from arthritis. *See* Arthritis
Hay fever, 158-59
HDL cholesterol, 17-18, 143-45
Head lice, 44-45
Headaches, 206-7
caused by menstruation, 220, 223
Heart attack. *See* Angina
Heartburn, 178-84
Hemp seed, 116-17
Herbal tea, for treating
acne and breakouts, 73
appetite loss, 217
asthma, 19
gas and bloating, 176
headaches, 207
heartburn, 182
hiccups, 29
menstrual cramps, 221
overweight, 134
stomach ache or pain, 185
vomiting and nausea, 194
weak immune system, 150
Hiccups, 29-30
High blood pressure, 31-33. *See also* Angina
High cholesterol, 15, 17-18, 143-45
Honey, 8, 18, 20-21, 59, 70, 77, 80, 83-85, 87, 89-90, 97, 105-6, 150, 153-154, 158, 179, 203, 212
Hyperpigmentation, 105-8
Hypertension. *See* High blood pressure
Hyperthyroidism. *See* Thyroid disease
Hypothyroidism. *See* Thyroid disease

I

IBS. *See* Inflammatory bowel syndrome
Ice, for relieving
  cuts and bruises, 81
  toothache, 56
Immune system, strengthening, 150-57
Incontinence, urinary. *See* Urinary incontinence
Indigestion. *See* Bloating; Gassiness; Heartburn; Nausea
Infections
  ear, 7
  eye, 8-11
  gum, 51-52
  sinus, 26-28, 206-7
  urinary tract, 189-90
Inflamed skin, 100-104
Inflammatory bowel syndrome. *See* Bloating; Constipation; Stomach cramps; Diarrhoea; Gassiness
Insect bites, 208-10
Insomnia, 211-16
Itching
  caused by
    bee stings, 209
    dry skin, 93-96
    eczema, 93-96
    insect bites, 208-10
  of eyes, as allergy symptom, 160

J

Joint pain, 112-23
Jojoba oil, 94

K

Knee pain. *See* Joint pain

L

Lavender oil, 23, 74-75, 206, 209, 214
LDL cholesterol. *See* High cholesterol
Lemon, 36-39, 129, 152, 169-70, 204-5
Lemongrass, 24-25, 27, 115-16
Lime, 32, 129, 169-70, 196, 204-5
Lips, chapped, 85-89
Liquorice root, 102-3, 107-8, 182
Loss of appetite. *See* Appetite, loss of
Lower-back pain. *See* Back pain

M

Massage
  for treating
    gum infection, 51
    hair loss and thinning, 43
    headache, 206
    muscle soreness or cramps, 126, 220
    stomach pain, 187-88
Menstrual cramps, 220-23
Migraines, 206-7
Milk, 15-16, 21, 27, 95, 136, 138, 153-54, 166, 178, 211-12, 222
Mint, 24-25, 27, 28, 150-51
Morning sickness. *See* Nausea
Motion sickness. *See* Nausea
Mouth ulcers. *See* Canker sores
Muscle cramps, 124-29
Muscle pain, 124-29
Muscle soreness, 124-29

N

Nasal congestion. *See* Congestion
Nasal drops, 26
Nausea, 194-198
Neck pain. *See* Joint pain; Muscle pain
Neem, 37-39, 44-45, 68-69, 94-95
Nits. *See* Head lice
Nose
  runny, *See* Congestion
  stuffy, *See* Congestion
Nutmeg, 97-98, 106-7

O

Oatmeal, 100-101
Obesity. *See* Overweight
Olive oil, 6, 23, 126, 139
Onion, 83
Orange peel, 105
Osteoarthritis. *See* Arthritis
Overactive bladder. *See* Urinary incontinence
Overactive thyroid. *See* Thyroid disease
Overweight, 132-35

P

Pain. *See* specific kinds
Papaya, 67, 86, 128
Paper cuts. *See* Cuts
Papules. *See* Acne
Peppermint oil, 74-75
Period, pain. *See* Menstrual cramps
Periodontitis. *See* Gum infection
Petroleum jelly, 159
Physical therapy, for arthritis, 119-23
Pimples
  acne, *See* Acne
  eyelid, *See* Chalazia
Pineapple, 82-83, 128-29
Pinkeye. *See* Conjunctivitis
Pistachio, 212-13
PMS. *See* Pre-menstrual syndrome
Pomegranate, 191
Poppy seed, 212-13
Pores, enlarged, 97-99
Potato, 91
Pranayama, for
  constipation, 165
  fatigue, 202
  high blood pressure, 31-32
  high cholesterol, 144-45
  immune system, strengthening, 156
  insomnia, 216
  joint pain or arthritis, 118
  thyroid disease, 146
Pre-menstrual syndrome (PMS)
  symptoms of
    acne or breakouts, 64-73
    bloating, 174-77
    constipation, 164-67
    fatigue, 202-5
    headache, 206-7, 220, 223
    insomnia, 211-16
    tummy pain, 220-23
Pressure point, for
  stomach ache or pain, 187
  thyroid disease, 147
  vomiting or nausea, 198
Prunes, 167
Psoriasis, 37, 39, 96, 103
Puffy eyes, 90-92
Pumpkin seed, 193

Q

Queasiness. *See* Nausea

R

Raisins, 150-51
Rashes, caused by
  eczema, 93-96
  insect bites, 208-10
Redness, skin, 100-104
Reflux. *See* Heartburn
Repetitive strain injury, 118. *See also* Joint pain
Rheumatoid arthritis. *See* Arthritis.
Rhinitis, allergic. *See* Congestion; Hay fever
Rice, 172-73
Rosacea, 103. *See also* Redness, skin
Rose water, 9-10, 65-66, 75-76, 95-96, 98, 99, 104
Runny nose. *See* Congestion

S

Saffron, 211-13, 222-23
Salt, 26, 54-55, 60, 139, 169-70, 204-5
Sandalwood, 65-67, 98, 106-7

Scalp
dandruff, 36-39
head lice, 44-45
massage, for hair loss, 43
psoriasis of, 37, 39
Scars, 105-8
Scrapes. *See* Bruises; Cuts
Seasickness. *See* Nausea
Seborrheic dermatitis
dandruff caused by, 37, 39
Sesame oil, 77-78
Shoulder pain. *See* Joint pain; Muscle pain
Sinus infection. *See* Sinusitis.
Sinusitis. *See* Congestion; Headache
Sinus problems
runny nose, 26-28
stuffy nose, 26-28
Skin problems
acne or breakouts, 64-73
burns, 74-78
corns and calluses, 79-80
cuts and bruises, 81-84
chapped or dry lips, 85-89
dark circles and puffy eyes, 90-92
dry skin, 93-96
enlarged pores, 97-99
redness and inflammation, 100-104
scars and hyperpigmentation, 105-108
Sleep problems
chronic fatigue syndrome, 202-3
fatigue, 202-5
insomnia, 211-16
Sleep deprivation. *See* Insomnia.
Sodium bicarbonate, 7, 175
Sore throat, 21-25
Steam, for treating
acne or breakouts, 64-65
congestion, 28
enlarged pores, 97
Stings. *See* Insect bites
Stomach ache, 185-88. *See also* Nausea
Stomach cramps, 185-88. *See also* Menstrual cramps
Stomach flu. *See* Stomach cramps; Diarrhoea; Vomiting
Stomach upset, 185-88. *See also* Nausea
Stretching, for joint or muscle pain, 119
Styes, on eye, 11
Stuffy nose. *See* Congestion
Sugar, 22, 85-86, 169-70, 204-5
Sunburn. See Burns

T

Tapioca, 172-73
Tea. *See* Herbal tea
Tea bag, for treating
acne, 71
mouth ulcers, 58
redness and inflammation, 102
Tea tree oil, 44-45, 209
Tendonitis. *See* Joint pain; Muscle pain
Tennis elbow. *See* Joint pain; Muscle pain
Throat, sore. *See* Sore throat
Throwing up. *See* Vomiting
Thyroid disease, 146-47
Tiredness. *See* Fatigue; Insomnia
Toothache, 53-56
Turmeric, 11, 16, 20-21, 51-52, 65, 81, 90, 94, 100, 106, 112, 125, 141, 150, 154, 158, 160, 203, 208, 220

U

Ulcers, mouth. *See* Canker sores
Underactive thyroid. *See* Thyroid disease
Underweight, 136-139
Upset stomach. *See* Nausea; Stomach cramps
Urinary incontinence, 191-93
Urinary retention, 193
Urinary tract infections (UTIs), 189-90
UTIs. *See* Urinary tract infections

V

Vaseline, 159
Vaporub. *See* Vicks
Vicks, 28, 127
Vomiting, 194-98

W

Watermelon, 32-33
Weak immune system, 150-57
Weight gain, for underweight, 136-139
Weight loss, for overweight, 132-35
Wheatgrass, 180-81
Whiteheads. *See* Acne
Wind. *See* Gassiness
Wound healing. *See* Cuts
Wrist pain. *See* Joint pain; Muscle pain

Y

Yoga, for
  gassiness and bloating, 177
  heartburn, 183
  high cholesterol, 144-45
  joint pain or arthritis, 119-23
  thyroid disease, 146
Yoghurt, 36, 65, 105-6, 138, 171-72

About the author

Tanika graduated from University College London with a First Class Honours in Management Science, and recently joined the consulting division of one of the big four professional services firms in London. Tanika's academic career has fostered a mindset of critical thinking and singular focus on the subjects that have attracted her attention so far. She has always delved deep into any area of interest, researching it thoroughly, until she accumulates the knowledge that provides her a comprehensive, in-depth perspective. Sometimes she arguably takes this approach too far, spending hours researching even basic purchases like toilet paper.

Being of Indian descent but born and raised in the UK, immersed in British culture, Tanika was always drawn to understanding more about her heritage - the Hindi language, Indian traditions, food, and alternative medicine. This also involved spending many hours with her grandmother who shared her ways of 80 years of healthy living. It was the combination of Tanika's curiosity and enthusiasm to share her learnings that gave birth to The Natural Remedy Lab.